BATTERSEA
PAST

First published 2002
by Historical Publications Ltd
32 Ellington Street, London N7 8PL
(Tel: 020 7607 1628)

ISBN 0 948667 76 1
British Library Cataloguing-in-Publication Data
A catalogue record for this book is available from the British Library

Typeset in Palatino by Historical Publications ltd
Reproduction by G & J Graphics, London EC2
Printed in Zaragoza, Spain, by Edelvives

The Illustrations

We are grateful to the following for their permission to reproduce illustrations.

Aero Films: *94*
Mike Bull: *the jacket*
Roger Cline: *1, 101, 126, 127*
Historical Publications: *3, 4, 7, 8, 9, 12, 13, 15, 21, 65, 75, 77, 83, 90, 103, 118, 122, 123, 124, 180*
Roger Logan: *25, 174, 175*
Patrick Loobey: *6, 22, 23, 24, 26, 27, 28, 29, 30, 32, 33, 34, 35, 36, 37, 38, 39, 40, 41, 42, 43, 45, 46,
47, 48, 49, 50, 51, 54, 55, 56, 57, 58, 59, 60, 61, 62, 66, 67, 68, 69, 71, 72, 73, 74, 76, 78, 79, 82,
85, 86, 88, 92, 93, 95, 96, 97, 98, 99, 100, 102, 104, 105, 106, 107, 108, 109, 110, 111, 112, 113, 114,
115, 116, 117, 119, 120, 128, 129, 131, 132, 134, 135, 136, 137, 138, 139, 141, 148, 149, 151, 153, 155,
157, 158, 159, 160, 162, 163, 164, 165, 167, 170, 171, 176, 177, 178, 179*
Wandsworth Local History Collection: *5, 10, 14, 16, 17, 18, 19, 20, 31, 44, 52, 80, 81, 84, 142, 143,
144, 145, 146, 147, 156, 168*
Wandsworth Museum: *2, 11, 53, 63, 64, 70, 87, 89, 91, 121, 125, 130, 133, 140, 150, 152, 154, 161,
169, 172, 173*

BATTERSEA PAST

Edited by Patrick Loobey

with contributions from
Keith Bailey, Sean Creighton, Rita Ensing, Tony Evans,
Pamela Greenwood, Roger Logan, Patrick Loobey
and R.A. Shaw

HISTORICAL PUBLICATIONS

Introduction

Modern Battersea began in the latter half of the 18th century when Earl Spencer bought title to the Manor of Wandsworth and Battersea, and commenced selling land to business and to speculators. Then the construction of a bridge to Chelsea in 1772 opened up trade to Battersea's riverside industries and these, especially at Nine Elms, soon took over the waterside.

Until the early 19th century most traffic to and from the village was carried on the Thames – even the dead were brought from Nine Elms by river and not by road. But the coming of the railway to Nine Elms in 1838 and the opening of the misnamed Clapham Junction station in 1863 was to end Battersea's isolation.

Agriculture was a major occupation up to the 1860s, with notices put up along what is now Battersea Park Road in the 1840s, to the effect that "Anyone found plucking an ear of Corn will be fined one shilling". The Falcon Brook was covered over, deepened and redirected by the Metropolitan Board of Works in 1865 so that traffic could pass safely along Battersea Rise and for building development to continue in the area of St John's Road and Northcote Road. Even so, farm animals still proved a nuisance to the new tenants of Webbs Road in the 1880s, as animals wandered in from local piggeries. Latchmere Road was known as Pig Hill well into the 20th century.

The railway yards and workshops at Nine Elms took up hundreds of acres and employed many hundreds of local residents, and a variety of industries along the Thames gave work to thousands, not only directly but in the support and servicing of these large factories – Thames lightermen, for example, and the transport of materials by barge to the London Docks.

Entertainment was often associated with the public houses, of which there were 207 before the end of the 19th century. Music halls attached to these were the earlier form of licensed entertainment, but purpose built theatres were erected in the 1890s, to be superseded by cinemas as soon as regular supplies of electricity could be generated in the following century.

Much of Battersea was built by private developers, but the Council, with its left-wing bias, allocated funds to build 'social housing' as soon as it was formed in 1900. The Council also provided baths, libraries and a direct labour workforce.

The Borough has a distinct lack of statues or memorials, no doubt due to the Council's lack of deference to Royalty or personalities; a few plaques have been attached to houses, and war memorials were erected in churches and in Battersea Park. The one exception is the farcical story of the little Brown Dog Statue erected in Latchmere Gardens in 1906 (*see p. 102*).

Battersea has one of the largest parks in any capital city, of 200 acres and can also lay claim to most of Clapham Common and a good portion of Wandsworth Common, both of which were secured for the public in the 1870s. The very small Latchmere Gardens (Latchmere Common in the 18th century) almost became the site for Battersea cemetery in the 1880s when the allotments were suggested as a suitable site.

Battersea suffered greatly during the Second World War for being home to so much industry, the many crossing points of the Thames, the railway yards, Clapham Junction and of course Battersea Power Station. These targets, with a few exceptions, were rarely disrupted but much nearby housing was reduced to rubble necessitating wholesale rebuilding of large areas in the 1950s and 1960s and the displacement of many residents from Battersea altogether, to Roehampton and elsewhere. There are probably more ex-residents of Battersea than the present population.

Many residents mourned the dismantling of the Borough Council in 1965 and its absorption into the London Borough of Wandsworth. The last meeting of the old council took place on 31 March 1965 followed on 8 May by the laying-up of the Borough Arms at a ceremony held at St Mary's parish church.

The greatest change to Battersea life, in the 1970s, was the removal of industry to Wales and the Midlands after the closure of the railway yards in the late 1960s and of Nine Elms gasworks about 1970. As their sites have been built on with office blocks and housing, so the emphasis of Battersea employment has changed to service industries using fewer staff.

The members of Wandsworth Historical Society who have written this book are: Keith Bailey (sections on the Anglo-Saxons, Victorian housing and society, schools, shops and transport); Rita Ensing (Medieval, with Keith Bailey); Dr Pamela Greenwood (geology and archaeology); Roger Logan (social and economic development from the 17th to 19th century and 20th-century council housing); Sean Creighton (Unions and politics); Patrick Loobey has edited the work and contributed material on entertainment, industry, churches, sport and public houses. Other contributions were made by Tony Evans and R.A. Shaw.

Early times

GEOLOGY

Battersea parish covers 2,315 acres (excluding 770 acres at Penge, which although part of Battersea until 1888, is not treated here), similar to Wandsworth, Streatham and Putney, larger than Clapham, but smaller than Lambeth and Camberwell. Geology has influenced its development, from the hills and steep slopes of Lavender Hill and the plateau of Clapham Common to the extensive low-lying former marshy areas alongside the Thames. The River Thames first made a course through the London Clay of the London area in the Anglian Glacial period (478-423,000 years ago). In cold periods during the rest of the Ice Age the Thames cut through the sands and gravels laid down in warmer periods, leaving the characteristic step-like formation of flat terraces and steep bluffs visible in the Lavender Hill area. Brickearth and alluvium were also deposited during warmer phases over the last 400,000 years with tributaries such as the Falcon and Effra pushing their way through these deposits. Battersea village lies on what was once an island, formed about 5,000 to 6,000 years ago.

There are four landscape units, defined by superficial geology and relief. The largest unit (57%) is the Thames Flood Plain Terrace. These gravels, loams and sands are the lowest terrace. The Flood Plain lies between 10-30ft. O.D., producing generally fertile soils, which formed the basis of Battersea's Common Field, covering c.400 acres east of the village. This fertility was the basis for commercial horticulture after 1600 – by 1800, Battersea was renowned for its asparagus and lavender. Parts of the Flood Plain were covered with loess, a fine wind-blown clayey loam, known as brickearth. As in many places in London, first-rate farmland also made good brickearth and several estates in Battersea evolved from market gardens. But local brickmaking occurred long before the Victorian era. In 1638-9, Robert Taylor was licensed to make 445,000 bricks at a kiln on Latchmere Common, of which 195,000 were used in rebuilding the tower of St. Mary's church. Most surviving pre-1800 houses in Battersea are brick-built, probably using local material.

A small area around Nine Elms and a strip along the river is formed from the most recent alluvial deposits (4-5% of the total). Essentially marshy, it was subject to flooding until embanked piecemeal from medieval times to the 1840s. Nine Elms was noted for its willows and generally Dutch aspect as late as the 1830s.

The third component is London Clay (12% overall, but rising to 22% in south-west Battersea). It is exposed in the slopes of the north-south Falcon brook valley, and in the prominent east-west bluff from Queenstown Road to Usk Road. This bluff divides north and south Battersea and generally areas of working class housing from those built for the middle classes. The embankment of the London & Southampton Railway, built across the Flood Plain in 1834-8, does not form a major social demarcation, despite its disruption of old lines of communication. Erosion has produced steep slopes 30-35ft. high, but despite this, they did not form a barrier to the Victorian builder. London Clay tends to be very heavy when wet and hard when dry and therefore not ideal for arable farming. Much of the clay was used for grazing and for the grounds of large houses before development.

The higher ground is covered by two further terrace deposits (27%), the Taplow and Boyn Hill Terraces, at about 45-60ft. and 80-100ft. O.D. respectively. They are an assortment of sands, gravels and loams, but longer erosion has rendered them less fertile and attractive for agriculture, especially the Boyn Hill deposits which underlie the extensive tracts of manorial waste (now Clapham and Wandsworth Commons). The northern part of the Taplow Terrace was enclosed early, and may never have been open field. These areas have long been regarded as the most salubrious, combining an elevated position with fine views over London and good natural drainage. Almost all of the mansions built after 1750 were around the commons, their estates not developed until after 1880.

In summary, the topography of Battersea may be likened to a 'T', in which the crossbar is the low-lying north of the parish, the site of the medieval village and its common field. The commercial horticulture, which developed after 1600, delayed widespread enclosure until the onset of house building from 1840. The downstroke is formed by the Falcon brook, whose valley is bounded by steep London Clay slopes capped by flat expanses of gravel. This area was sparsely settled before 1700, and not finally covered by the tide of suburban building until 1914.

1. *Part of John Rocque's map of Surrey, published in 1760, showing Battersea and its hinterland to the south.*

ARCHAEOLOGY

The early Palaeolithic period (400,000 to 40,000 years ago) is represented by a few flint tools and hand axes abraded by river or glacial action found in the Thames and from the St John's Hill and Battersea Rise area.

Traces of the Mesolithic era (13,000 to 10,000 years ago) are more plentiful, particularly from the Thames and its foreshore. Finds include antler harpoons for spearing fish, bone points and awls, flint axes and adzes for tree-felling and carpentry, an antler sleeve for an axe plus a number of flint tools for the everyday tool kit. The river levels have altered to such an extent that the occupation and activity areas may be buried or submerged. The Neolithic period (4,500-2,200 BC) introduced a more settled farming economy with the use of pottery and different styles of flint tools. The sparse evidence from Battersea is some pottery, several types of stone axe, an antler comb, and flint tools, all from the Thames foreshore, plus one flint axe from Battersea Rise. For the Bronze (2,400-800BC) and Iron Ages (800-50BC) there are plenty of objects but settlements have still to be found. A fine battle-axe, a spearhead and several flat-axes, from the Thames, represent the early Bronze Age. In common with other Thameside areas in the London region, there are rich finds of prestige bronze weapons and other objects, comprising rapiers, leaf-shaped swords and a sheet bronze cauldron now on display in the British Museum. The Iron Age river finds include swords, some in scabbards, daggers, a harness fitting and two pots containing human bones. The most famous archaeological object from the area is the Battersea shield, a sheet bronze parade shield decorated with red glass found during work on Chelsea Bridge. The Roman period has left little evidence except for a few fragments of pottery and building material found in Battersea Square that may indicate field scatter from a settlement nearby. Roman artefacts discovered on the river and foreshore at Battersea Reach are most likely dumped materials from construction of the London docks in the 19th century. Towards the end of the Roman period (300-400 AD) there was clearly a sophisticated settlement in Battersea with an individual able to afford a finely decorated lead coffin. This was found in 1794 in Battersea Fields, alongside three more skeletons without coffins. The lead coffin, only 4ft 10ins long, may have been for a child.

The possibility of Roman life continuing into

2. *The Iron Age Battersea Shield.*

what is termed the Saxon era is from the twelve lead ingots dredged up at Battersea. The ingots are stamped with the Chi-Rho symbol and the words *Spes in Deo; XP* (Hope in God; Christ). The name SYAGRIVS has been found on two recent samples. These may date to the late 4th or 5th century, Syagrius possibly being a King or Bishop of that name. The field name 'Walworth Shot' (from Old English words meaning 'enclosure of the Britons or slaves'), near the High Street, may refer to the presence of native British people during the Saxon period. Fifth century and later Saxon stray finds include seaxes (knives), a late Saxon stirrup and a Viking sword and axe. One of the seaxes, probably 8th-century, has a runic alphabet or *futhorc* scratched on it, as well as the name Beagnoth, its maker and/or owner. The first direct evidence for a settlement or farmstead is the archaeological excavation at Althorpe Grove where traces of rectangular post-built timber buildings, dating to the middle Saxon period (*c*.650-850) were uncovered.

UNDER THE ANGLO-SAXONS

The first appearance of Battersea in the documentary record is in two Anglo-Saxon charters, one of which is merely a list of boundary marks. Both offer difficulties of interpretation. The first is dated 693, but survives only in a late-11th century copy, which has been altered to reflect the then ownership of the estate by Westminster Abbey. The charter records the granting of a 68-hide estate, by Eorcenweald, Bishop of London (675-693), some time in the 680s. (A hide was notionally the land needed to support one family group, and varied in size dependent upon the quality of the land.) The beneficiary was the double monastery which he had founded at Barking in Essex, presided over by his sister Ethelburga. Three areas are named: Battersea (Batrices ege), with 28 hides; Washingham (Watsingaham – 'settlement of Wathsige's [people), twenty hides, and a further twenty hides by the Hidaburna (probably the Wandle [Anglo-Saxon hlyd burna, 'loud stream'], but possibly the Falcon Brook, originally Hydeburn). The derivation of Battersea's name is thought to be 'Beaduric's island, or raised ground in a marsh', an apt description of the site of the old village. J.G. Taylor, in his book *Our Lady of Batersey* (1925), lists 70 different spellings of the name from 693 to 1597. The modern spelling first appears in 1595.

Large grants of land are typical of the early years of the conversion of the Anglo-Saxons to Christianity, and include several settlements and their resources. Eorcenweald was closely associated with the kingdoms contending for control of the London area (Kent, Essex, Wessex and Mercia), and one of their rulers probably gave him the estate prior to his granting it to Barking Abbey. The charter witnesses include Athelred of Mercia (675-704), overlord to Cædwalla of Wessex (685-8), who was probably Eorcenweald's benefactor.

'Battersea' is the northern part of the parish, bounded by the Thames, Heathwall Sewer and Falcon Brook. Washingham survived as a name into the 1820s, and refers to the area between the two commons around the Rise. The settlement was located on or close to the line of a probable Roman road, running from Stane Street at Clapham towards Wandsworth and Putney. The remainder of the estate was eastern Wandsworth, as far as the Wandle, which was linked with Battersea administratively for a thousand years.

A boundary perambulation is appended to the charter, probably of the tenth century, as is a second list of about 957, which has no associated grant. The estate concerned was larger than that given to Barking Abbey, and was later acquired by Westminster, including the whole of Wandsworth and Putney, and parts of Wimbledon, Balham and Tooting. Insofar as Battersea is concerned, the boundary follows that of the later parish in the east, starting at the Thames. The first point is 'High Bank' (OE *heah yfre* [693]; *hegefre* [957]), which may refer either to a natural shore of the Thames and/or its now-covered tributary the Effra, or to an early man-made embankment to protect the low-lying marshes from flooding. Next comes *ceokan ege* [693], 'the island or raised ground of a man called Ceacca, or shaped like a cheek', or *gaeteneshaele* [957], 'a nook/corner frequented by young goats'. These points may or may not have been the same, but lay somewhere along the line of the Heathwall Sewer, perhaps in the vicinity of the present Silverthorne Road. The next mark is *gryddeles elrene* [693] or *gryndeles syllen* [957], respectively 'Grendel's alder[s]' and 'Grendel's bog'. Grendel of course was the monster in the epic poem Beowulf, who quite often gave his name to watery landscape features, especially marshes or bogs. This feature seems likely to have been where the Battersea-Clapham boundary turns sharply south-west of Queenstown Road, at the foot of a steep slope where water may well have collected. The 'small oak' (*smalan ac*, 693 only) probably grew where the boundary crossed the Roman road now represented by North Side. Rushmere (*rysmere* [693]; *ryssemere* [957]) will have been a pond on Clapham Common, probably in the vicinity of South Side/Nightingale Lane. Thereafter, the charters diverge from the modern parish boundaries, to include parts of Balham and are later known as Clapham Detached, although it is possible that 'Bernard's burials' (*bernneardes byriels* [693]; *bernardes byrieles* [957], perhaps a group of prehistoric or Anglo-Saxon burial mounds, marked the point in Trinity Road where the extreme southern point of Battersea lies between Wandsworth and Streatham parishes.

Medieval Battersea

MANOR AND MILLS

The manor of Battersea and its berewick (literally 'barley farm', but here denoting an outlying portion of a manor) of Wandsworth were granted to St Peter's Abbey, Westminster (today's Westminster Abbey) in 1067 by William the Conqueror in exchange for Windsor where he wished to create a forest for hunting. The Domesday entry of 1086 for Battersea also includes the tolls from Wandsworth (probably boat landing fees) and from seven watermills, probably on the River Wandle, the Falcon Brook not having sufficient force, although there may have been mills worked by the Thames.

There was land for seventeen ploughs on the combined manor, possibly denoting 1,700 acres of arable. Three ploughs were on the lord's private land (demesne) (*cf.* 425 acres of demesne arable in 1300-30). The population in 1086 comprised forty-five villeins (tenant farmers), sixteen bordars or smallholders with eight slaves, who would have operated the ploughs on the demesne and probably some of the mills. These figures suggest a total population of 300-320. In King Edward's time (1066) the manor was worth £80 but in 1067 had fallen to £30, probably an indication of the devastation caused by William the Conqueror's march around London. By 1086, however, it had recovered to £75 9s 8d, of which no less than £42 9s 8d was from the mills, making them the most valuable mills in England – kept busy no doubt supplying the already insatiable demands of the London market. Eighty-two acres of meadowland are mentioned together with pannage or payment of one hog in ten to the Abbot at Westminster.

The western limit of the manor was the River Wandle. Because the monks at Westminster regarded the area as one manor, it is not always possible to separate the history of Battersea from that of Wandsworth. In 1176-88 the manor was assigned to the infirmary at Westminster. In 1225

3. Mills by the Battersea riverside and on the Falcon brook survived well into the 19th century. Here depicted is a corn mill and the Red House, well known for its entertainments.

4. Randall's mill at Nine Elms is shown here in a water colour by John Varley in 1830.

Abbot Richard de Berking made a formal partition of the Abbey's many manors into those which maintained himself and his household, and those for the maintenance of the Prior and Convent of monks and for the Abbey church. Battersea and Wandsworth now came under the Prior and Convent, which the monks considered as one of their five principal manors, lying as it did only a couple of miles by river from the abbey.

A customal made at the time of the 1225 partition names six separate settlements. Battersea and Wandsworth were both by the Thames on their present sites; Hese (OE 'brushwood') was further east by the Thames, near the present Nine Elms; Washingham covered the high ground to the south bordering on Clapham; Bruges (later Bridges) lay between Battersea and Wandsworth by the Thames on the north and the main highway to the south. A further hamlet was Roydon ('rye hill'), centred on St John's Hill around the Plough Inn.

An important early tenant was Richard de Dol who acquired land in Battersea and Wandsworth in 1200, and held more in Bridges and Roydon.

A stone wharf at Bridges on the site of the later York House *(see p. 13)* was used in 1204 for shipping Reigate stone for use at the Royal castle at Windsor and in 1218 for the supply of stone for Waltham Abbey. A *Porta*, or landing stage, was built at Battersea in 1297/8 for transhipping stone from Westerham to Westminster. This wharf was mentioned in 1368/9 for transporting timber and in 1365 when Reigate stone was shipped to Hadleigh Castle in Essex.

MANOR CUSTOMS

The distinction between free and customary (villein) tenants was always strictly maintained by the monks. About 1268, Hese had four customary tenants holding four virgates (60 acres). There were nine virgates (135 acres) of customary land at Wassingham and 6½ virgates (98 acres) at Bridges. By 1312, 40 tenants held less than ten acres or less of arable land, who could only be called smallholders and 25 held between ten and twenty acres; two only had over thirty acres. The labour services and the cash due, in addition to rent, from a customary tenant like John Colman, who held a house and one virgate of 15 acres, were onerous. He paid twelve pence rent at Michaelmas, seven pence on St Martin's day (11 November) and at the old festival of Hoke Day (2nd Tuesday after Easter) one bushel of corn worth five pence. He also had to give one day's labour a week and with the other tenants to do seasonal work such as ploughing, harrowing, threshing rye for winter sowing and ploughing at Lent. They also did a number of other works such as weeding, lifting and stacking hay. For these services there was a carefully prescribed amount of food at the lord of the manor's table – bread, soup, cheese, meat, or fish and ale. A licence from the lord was also required to marry off a son or daughter.

A list of taxpayers in Battersea from 1332 names twenty-six individuals paying a total of £2 4s.4d; most paid less than one shilling, but Robert le Dol, descendant of Richard, paid 10/-. The abbot's tenants are listed separately. There were sixteen of them paying only 10s 3d, most only 1d. or 2d. They included Walter of Hese.

The Manor House close to the present St Mary church site, described as a capital messuage with a *placca* or square was worth 6s 8d per year; it had a garden of three acres which produced fruit and vegetables worth 8s and a dovecote worth 3s. The effects of the Black Death of 1348/9 were a shortage of labour and a fall in land prices whereupon the Abbey repurchased much land lost in the 12th century. In 1366 the Battersea ploughmen supplied three ploughs to help in the rest of Wandsworth. In 1368 there was a massive supply from Battersea of seed corn and no less than 377 sheep. Simon Clerk, the sergeant, sent his corn in 1372 to be ground at Adkyn's mill in Wandsworth and in the same year received 74,000 plain tiles from the kiln at Allfarthing.

In 1374, Robert Brown, the Battersea sergeant, received 88,000 plain and 900 ridge tiles for some extensive building operation taking place in Battersea. Battersea and Wandsworth Manor had been managed by a succession of officials of different types, a reeve, beadle or sergeant, but from the beginning of the 15th century it was leased to a 'farme' for a fixed rent. The Rydon family, prominent in Battersea, was a part of this. John Rydon was beadle in 1379 and reeve in the early 1390s. Another family member, Stephen Rydon, had been sergeant of Doune Manor in Wandsworth in the 1390s. Throughout the 15th century the family leased the manor and a descendant married Oliver St John in the 16th century when the connection of the St John family with Battersea began.

5. *The height of the earthen riverside wall, near the Red House is noticeable, with a small cottage to the right below the embankment, date c.1800*

6. *Flooding of the Thames at Nine Elms; from the Illustrated London News 13 January, 1877.*

7. *The 18th-century York House. The land was still owned by the Archbishop of York until late that century, but it had been let out since the 16th century.*

8. *The site of York House near the bridge across the river Hidaburna.*

THE RIVER WALL

A river wall was maintained by Battersea residents to keep out the many inundations from the Thames. Floods are mentioned in 1483,1489/90, 1570 and later in 1774 and 1875. Making the Thames bank in 1534-5 took seven men eleven days and cost £2. Three years earlier the monk bailiff's barn had been repaired at a cost of 17s 6d, including tiles, lathes, lime and sand. Repairs to the gatehouse by the river cost 12s 10d – virtually the last expenditure undertaken in Battersea by the monks.

A notable tenant of the manor was Laurence Booth, Bishop of Durham, who in the 1460s purchased Bruges, an area which straddled both Battersea and Wandsworth parishes by the Thames, the name of which derived from a bridge over the mouth of the Falcon Brook. A house called Bridge Court was to be enclosed by walls and towers and the land imparked with rights to keep rabbits and to hunt. Booth, who in 1457, became Archbishop of York, bequeathed Bruges to the see of York and it became a separate manor. A later Archbishop of York, Robert Holgate, was committed to the Tower by Queen Mary in 1553. Troops sent to seize him rifled his house at Battersea and are said to have carried off £300 worth of gold coin, 1,600 ounces of plate, a mitre of gold set with very fine diamonds, sapphires and balists, other stones and pearls, some very valuable rings, the Archbishop's seal in silver and his signet ring, an antique in gold.

YORK HOUSE

In the reign of Edward IV (1461-83), Laurence Booth, later to become Archbishop of York, bought 400 acres by the riverside which he later annexed to the see of York. Here he built a house which became a residence for future archbishops on their visits to London. It was little used and, indeed, would not have been an attractive alternative to the York House acquired in the Strand in the next century.

Price's Candle factory was later built across the site of the house.

In Stuart times

As James I ascended to the throne in 1603, Battersea was at the beginning of a period of transition. Over the next century, greater diversity in land usage altered the appearance of the parish. While remaining pre-eminently open and agricultural, the rural landscape was affected by the trend around London for market gardening – the Battersea soil proved well suited to the growing of vegetables. Industrial and manufacturing areas developed, particularly along the Thames. Increasingly, former agricultural land was built over, some to form both large estates and compressed pockets of residential developments.

POPULOUS AREAS

As a consequence, by the mid-17th century the parish, for the purpose of poor rate assessment, became defined by localities.

The central area, 'Battersey neere the Church', was that portion of the village lying to the south of St Mary's church as far as Battersea Square, including the Manor House standing to the east of the church. The evidence suggests that by the middle of the century this was a mixed residential and trading district. One inhabitant was a baker, Robert Crosse, who was summoned in 1661 to appear at Surrey Quarter Sessions for "selling loaves being less than the true and just assize". Close by lived Henry Cock, a carpenter, also brought to account. His alleged crime was to have "caused a great quantity of wood to be placed in the highway leading from Battersea to the parish church". Joseph Fo(o)rd, a waterman, was summonsed in 1662 for "not having repaired to [his] parish church nor to any other usual place of common prayer for three months." A local inn-keeper, John Soale, was named amongst those "fitt to be supprest" during the puritan days of 1653, although indications are that he was still in business in 1667. Strategically placed along what is now the western end of Battersea Church Road, tradesmen and craftsmen were in the prime location for anyone using the principal entrance to the village, the landing place hard by the church.

At the cross roads of routes heading to the points of the compass was 'the Elmes.' Later to be called Battersea Square, here stood three substantial properties together with some less significant properties. To the east of the Square, along today's Westbridge Road, was 'the

townfeild gate' close to which were parishioners occupying, on the whole, modestly rated properties. From the gate, a track across open fields led to 'the Ferrey place', at a site later to see the construction of Battersea Bridge (a ferry across the Thames to Chelsea had been instituted at the end of the 16th century). Local residents here included Hugh Phelps, a surname later to be associated with the history of the Thames at Putney.

Another principal area of occupation was described as 'the Pound to the Elmes', that is Battersea High Street from its junction with York Road to the Square. Rateable values suggest a wide range of property types.

'Nutt Lane to Yorke Place' refers to Lombard Road as far as the Falcon Brook. This was the second most prestigious area, if property assessments are considered. 'Yorke Place', was the vicinity of today's Candle Shop, and included York House the one time home of the Archbishops of York (*see p.13*).

A sparsely developed area was 'the Ryse to the Pound', today's Falcon Road. 'From the Pound to Yorke Place' was the stretch of York Road from the top of Battersea High Street to the Falcon Brook. 'Long hedge and Nine Elms' lay two miles distant from the High Street across the open common field. The long hedge, abutting Nine Elms Lane, was about 800 yards in length and formed the northern boundary of the farm to which it gave it's name.

PLAGUES

The parish was visited by outbreaks of plague on several occasions during the 17th century. The plague that affected London in 1636 also touched Battersea. One family, that of Robert Nutt, lost four daughters and a son. In 1644, 23 people were noted in the Battersea Churchwardens' accounts as dying of the plague and special purchases were made, such as "thre whole deale boards and a halfe that was used to carry the ancient folkes to church that dyed of the plague" and "a hand barough that was made to carry the dead folkes to church upon", an additional parish expenditure of £3 3s 7d.

The 1665 epidemic in London, the Great Plague, was much more devastating. That year 113 burials are recorded in the parish registers, though not all were plague victims. (The annual average in the 1670s and 1680s was between 65-70.) The outbreak took hold in July when there were 17 burials; these increased to 22 in August, to 28 in September and reduced to 16 in October. Several families lost three, even four, members. Within six weeks the Callindine family lost father, mother, son and daughter. The cost to the parish was ten times that of the 1644 outbreak, some £30 18s 9d, the most expensive item being the manufacture of coffins by Thomas Cock, which cost £4 12s 0d.

PARISH ADMINISTRATION
Effective control of local issues lay in the hands of the two Churchwardens. These men were selected annually by a small group of residents, including the Vicar, the outgoing and incoming Churchwardens and a limited number of other ratepayers. The Vestry itself met only once a year, around Easter time, to elect two Churchwardens and other officers for the ensuing year and to audit the accounts of the outgoing office holders. Increasingly the Churchwardens undertook civil functions. As early as 1578 their role had been defined as "Wardens or keepers of the Rentes goodes and ornaments of the parishe churche of Batersey in the Countie of Surrey for one whole yeare endinge at the ffeaste of Easter 1579 as also for all somes of money by them receyved & laid out for the use of same parishe in the said year."

Reporting to the Churchwardens were the Collectors of the Poor, Parish Constables and Surveyors of the Highways. The role of the Collectors changed after 1601, with administration of the Poor Law passing into the hands of annually elected Overseers of the Poor. These were local residents nominated by the County Justices of the Peace to levy and collect a mandatory rate from householders and dispense financial benefit to those deemed to be in need. Instances of continued direct support for the poor show that voluntary legacies and donations supplemented the formal process. In 1634, for example, £3 9s 0d was paid to "a certain number of the poore in the greate froste."

Henry Cowper is the first recorded Constable, in 1608, although references to the office extend back as far as 1560. He and others who occupied the position during the 17th century dealt with a range of matters that included the duty of 'Watch and ward', the maintainence of the parish armour and the collection and delivery of money to help fund the Surrey County Gaol at St Margaret's Hill, Southwark. Known by its earlier name of the White Lyon, a reference to its former use as an inn, the gaol was in use up until the middle of the 17th century. Other duties of the Constable included the relief and transfer of licensed vagrants and making payments for the support of hospitals in the county.

The Surveyors of the Highway were also responsible for the upkeep of the "Town ffield Gates", situated either side of where Christchurch was built in the 19th century. The earliest mention of them is in 1560 when the records refer to the "Makinge of the two towne gates" and only six years later we have "pd to a Carpenter ffor a day worke abowte Ye towne ffeylde gates". The gates must have taken a battering for in 1570 both of them were renewed. Until the harvest was carried, the tenants had the right to close these gates, but they were thrown open for common grazing purposes until the end of November.

EARNING A LIVING
Opportunities for employment diversified immensely during the 17th century. The market gardens were labour intensive, and the increasing number of manufacturing premises created new occupations. Along what we know as Lombard Road, John Smith operated a sugar refinery. Around 1662, he began importing sugar from Barbados, where he had lived as a young man, establishing a family business that lasted well into the 18th century. Employment in such an industry was dangerous, sugar houses being exceptionally susceptible to fire. A contemporary outbreak in similar premises in the City was said to have caused a total loss of £70,000. Empathy locally resulted in Battersea's inhabitants contributing £4 2s 11d by way of a collection.

MIGRATION AND SETTLEMENT
Local concern about controlling potential settlers manifested itself in 1616. The Churchwardens and Overseers of the Poor, "wth ye ayd of ye constables" were required to undertake an examination of all incomers. The removal of those requiring support was a regular feature. Included in this category were pregnant women who, having no settlement rights in the parish, were helped on their way.

Immigration from Europe is indicated in a Return of Aliens in 'Battrichsey' dated 1599 in which Pieter Decollowaie and Sara, his wife, are mentioned. In 1656 Peter Decalloway junior was living in the High Street.

MANORIAL OWNERSHIP

The St John's, Lords of the Manor from 1627 to 1763, came into the area, as we have seen, through the marriage in 1593 of Oliver St John to Joan Holecroft, (daughter of Henry Roydon, also spelt Rydon), a widow who held a lease of the Manor from the Crown.

Oliver St John's career included being a Member of Parliament for Cirencester in 1592 before being knighted in 1599. In 1601 he went to Ireland to participate in the suppression of the rebellion led by Tyrone, subsequently holding the offices of Master of the Ordnance, Vice President of Connaught, Commissioner for the Plantation of Ulster, eventually, in 1616, becoming Lord Deputy of Ireland. He was created Viscount Grandison of Limerick Co. Leitrim in Ireland, returning to England in 1622. In 1626 he was made an English peer, Baron Tregoze of Highworth in Wiltshire, the following year obtaining a lease of the Manor of Battersea from the Crown in 1627. Three years later, on 29 December 1630, he died.

He left no children, the Manor passing to his nephew and heir Sir John St John who maintained a principal residence in Wiltshire and did not make a permanent home at Battersea. During the English revolution he supported the Royalist cause, whilst others of his family, notably his sister, aligned themselves with the Parliamentarians. He died in 1648.

Sir John was succeeded by his son Walter St John who, together with his brother, Henry and their respective wives, settled in Battersea Manor House on the bank of the Thames. In 1656 Walter succeeded to the title and family estates in Wiltshire and over the next fifty years played a useful and positive role in the life of Battersea. From 1675 some cottages at the southern end of the High Street were made available at a nominal rent to the Churchwardens for use as almshouses. At the turn of the century he established a charity to erect and endow a school for twenty free scholars. Thirty-one acres of land were purchased in Camberwell to produce the necessary income and the Rev. Nathaniel Gower was appointed the first master. Sir Walter's wife of 56 years, Lady Joanna, died in 1704 and four years later, at the age of 87, Sir Walter died.

Henry St John, his eldest son, followed Sir Walter as Lord of the Manor. In 1715 he became a peer with the title Viscount St John and Baron of Battersea. In contrast to his father, Henry St John made little contribution to local life. With his second wife, Angelica, he lived in the manor

9. *Sir Walter St John, Lord of Battersea Manor, who took a positive role in local life.*

house, which had started to decay. She died in 1736, leaving Henry to survive alone until 1742 when, aged 90, he died.

CIVIL WAR LOYALTIES

The impression conveyed by J.G. Taylor in his 1925 book *Our Lady of Batersey* is that the people of Battersea, "in its remote bend of the river", were in the main loyal to the King. In fact, its vicar of the period, Dr Thomas Temple, was one of the most prominent and active members of the Westminster assembly, an institution charged with reforming the Church of England. Temple came to Battersea in 1634, his appointment being made by Sir John St John, Lord of the Manor. His connections with the St John family went back to an Irish background where he had gone to Trinity College, Dublin.

The Georgian era

The accession of George III in 1760 was followed shortly afterwards by a change in the ownership of Battersea Manor. In 1763 the executors of Sarah, Duchess of Marlborough, added Battersea with Wandsworth Manor to their expanding portfolio of properties. In this way the Spencer family succeeded the St John's as principal landowners and landlords and this acted as a catalyst for change in both the topography and social structure of the area, particularly in central and south Battersea.

Earl Spencer disposed of an extensive acreage of agricultural land, some outright freehold, some on lease, to prospering businessmen, bankers and City gentlemen. The fields to the north and west of Battersea, and those on the perimeter of Battersea East (Clapham) Common, were transformed into modest landed estates that were themselves increasingly sub-divided as the century progressed. Along the eastern perimeter of Battersea West (Wandsworth) Common, five new

11. The Vicarage in 1826, former home of the Arctic explorer Edward Adrian Wilson in the 1890s and now St Mary's House, Vicarage Crescent.

houses were built, with pleasure grounds containing landscaped gardens and walks. Initially called Five Houses Lane, the road was later renamed Bolingbroke Grove.

In terms of social composition the effect of this

10. Eighteenth-century houses in Westbridge Road, demolished in 1957.

12.   The riverside at Battersea in 1742. The Manor House is to the left of St Mary's church, with its own stairs leading to the Thames.

suburban development was to introduce occupiers of status to Battersea. This was significant for the subsequent developments that were to take place, such as the building of Battersea Bridge and the rebuilding of the parish church of St Mary's. Taylor in his book on Battersea in 1925 refers to the increased carriage trade at the parish church and while there remained a substantial element of 'old' Batterseans, predominantly in the agricultural sector, new professions and trades started to appear. The former category contained such people as Benjamin Stables, Daniel Carter, and the father and son of the same name Henry Monger, all of whom were market gardeners during the 1760s and 1770s with family connections reaching back into Battersea's past. James Curry, between 1773 and 1789 described variously as a timber merchant and ship breaker, was indicative of the change occurring in the population. Others included Charles Craig, a pump borer, Urban Alderton, an auctioneer, and William Pindar, stonemason. The names of many who were to leave a mark on subsequent generations through the use of their surnames for road naming, lived and worked in Battersea at this period. Amongst these, Charles Wix, William and Robert Dent and Thomas Ponton are readily identifiable. One of the more unusual trades of local residents was that of a mole catcher.

Significantly, there were many other newcomers described not by profession or trade but as either gentleman or esquire. Christopher Baldwin became the occupier (and possibly the freehold owner) of the first of the new houses that were built around the western perimeter of the East Common. This was in the early 1760s. Described as 'esquire', he was a Surrey Justice of the Peace. On the northern boundary of the common at the same period lived Isaack Ackerman, a London businessman. While living at Battersea Rise House, he built the pair of houses on Clapham Common, North Side, about 1763, called The Sisters, one of which survives as Gilmore House on the corner of Elspeth Road. He served as a member of the St Mary's church rebuilding committee in the 1770s. Baldwin and Ackerman were examples of men who moved into and stayed in the parish for twenty or more years.

Towards the end of the century, members of the group later to be dubbed the 'Clapham Sect' lived in south Battersea; Henry Thornton occupied Battersea Rise House and William Wilberforce, Broomfield House.

13. Old houses at Nine Elms.

THE FIRST BATTERSEA BRIDGE

The construction of a permanent bridge across the Thames, linking the parish with Chelsea and a route to the expanding West End of London was undertaken in 1771. Financed by investments of £1000 each from fifteen proprietors, the bridge was made of wood with tollgates at both ends. The opening ceremony in November 1771 for foot passengers only was a splendid occasion, being recorded in contemporary newspaper accounts.

"Yesterday the new bridge was opened from Battersea to Chelsea amidst the concourse of many thousand people. At noon the bridge was crowded with people from one end to the other, in expectation of seeing the ceremony of its being opened which was as follows, viz.: a large number of workmen to clear the way; two foremen to measure the bridge which appeared to be 759 feet from one toll gate to the other, two toll collectors, the Clergymen of Battersea; the churchwardens of ditto; Surveyors of the highway of ditto; Overseers of the Poor; the clergymen, Churchwardens and Overseers of the Poor of Chelsea, Proprietors of the bridge two by two, the Treasurer, servants belonging to the gentlemen. When they arrived at the middle of the bridge, several pieces of cannon were fired and the bells of both parishes set to

ringing. The procession went to the Middlesex side and returned back again to the ferry house at Battersea, where an elegant entertainment was provided for them, Lord Spencer having presented the gentlemen with a doe upon the occasion."

Although opened, the bridge was not fully complete, being only boarded. The final surface of a thick coat of chalk, overlain with gravel, was applied later, and the bridge was opened for carriage traffic the following year. Despite this direct route to the north side of the river, development in Battersea was still slow to come.

BATTERSEA NEW TOWN

Towards the end of the 18th century one substantial speculative building scheme did begin, to be known as Battersea New Town.

At the eastern end of Battersea, building began in 1790 on former farmland abutting the south side of the main west-east route between Wandsworth and Lambeth. The reasons for its development remain obscure. Keith Bailey, in his investigation of this settlement, suggests connections with conditions arising out of the wars with France, which spanned the period 1792 to 1815, and the expansion of the built-up area south of

14. *The old wooden bridge at Battersea. The parish church is on the right, and the tall cylindrical structure was the Horizontal Air Mill; published in 1804.*

15. *The tollgates on Battersea Bridge in 1839.*

16. *Single storey houses in Stewarts Lane shortly before demolition c.1930.*

17. *Construction of a new wall and railings, at the corner of Battersea Park Road and Savona Street. This bridge is often referred to as 'The Dogs' Home Bridge' as the home is near where the chimney stands. It is viewed from Battersea New Town, which is to the left and behind the photographer.*

18. Houses in York Place, Battersea New Town. View from the Dogs' Home Bridge, c.1890.

the Thames as Georgian London advanced out into Surrey. Overall the 'New Town' took more than 80 years to be fully developed, though during the fifty years between 1790 and 1840 about one-third of the eventual total of some 432 houses were built. These were concentrated along Battersea Park Road, York Street (renamed Savona Street in 1871), New Street (Thessaly Road 1871) and Sleaford Street.

A minimal expansion of the existing village accompanied the New Town development. In west Battersea a modest development of small terraced housing did take place in York Road, to the west of York House, between 1770 and 1790. The area was becoming increasingly industri-alised and in the forty small cottages we may see signs of workers' housing being deliberately constructed.

INDUSTRIALISATION
The accessibility of Battersea from the Thames made stretches of its riverside attractive to manufacturers and by the end of the 18th century the frontage from Nine Elms to the Millpond was lined with small enterprises. At the western end

of the parish, land lying between the Thames and Lombard Road had long been commercially used.

THE CONTINUATION OF RURAL LIFE
But Battersea remained overwhelmingly a rural, agricultural parish throughout this period. This is borne out by comparing the three known maps of the period. The 'Crace' map of 1762 depicts a detailed field layout of north Battersea, all still recognisable in the Tithes redemption map of 1834. The names of the shots, furlongs, the field and farm boundaries, all combine to suggest a picture of an unchanging world. Some measure of change in the intervening period is apparent from the John Corris map of 1787. On this the large Millpond at Nine Elms is shown, and the bridge, replacing the ferry, is clearly marked.

It was not only in physical terms that Battersea remained locked in to the past. There is evidence for the survival of the medieval manorial system, with its associated features of deference and sub-jugation. The arrival of a new lord of the manor did not result in the reform of the process of allocating landholdings in the agricultural areas of the parish and transactions relating to these

19. *A single storey terrace including the Old Red House and Pavilion Tavern, Stewarts Lane, shortly before demolition c.1934.*

20. *The Royal Laundry, Westbridge Road c.1937. The 18th-century house was saved and refurbished after its neighbours were demolished in the 1970s.*

continued to be conducted in the Manorial Court Baron or Customary Court.

In 1787 the business before the Court was conducted by 'the Homage' so called because it was a jury of tenants owing homage to the lord of the manor. Their role was to consider 'present-ments' or requests to take up landholdings and ensure that the process was carried out according to custom. They also heard various pleas and actions brought to the Court. The timelessness of these is evident from the following examples.

"The Homage order that no person dig Sand Gravel or Turf from Battersea Common without the licence of the Lord. That the Pound keeper do take care thereof and take for each Cart load threepence and for each hundred feet of turf, sixpence."

"The Homage present that if any owner of swine shall suffer the same to go loose without being rung they shall forfeit for each swine the sum of two shillings and sixpence."

Meeting places for the Manorial Courts of Battersea with Wandsworth varied. In 1787 business began in the old Manor House by St Mary's church, before adjourning to the Star and

21. A room inside the Manor House – described as the "Roome wainscotted with ceader" and as "Pope's Parlour", was sold off and taken to America.

Garter public house opposite. The last recorded meeting place was the Spread Eagle in Wandsworth High Street in 1833 although the courts appear to have functioned until after the disposal of the majority of Spencer freeholds. As late as 1849, a Court Baron was held at which Eliza Gaines surrendered ownership of some land to Samuel Poupart, in consideration of the sum of 'Thirty Pounds of lawful money".

POPULATION
In 1801 the first population census in England was attempted. Carried out by local officials, the number of Battersea residents was found to be 3,365. The majority were described as being engaged in agricultural activity, with the greater part of the remainder involved in industry. For those earning sufficient to make it worthwhile insuring themselves against sickness, the rapidly spreading local friendly societies offered financial benefits. In Battersea there were friendly or amicable societies meeting in 1794 at the Nag's Head and the Swan, the former having been founded in 1777. A third friendly society, established in 1798, was by 1808 meeting at the Raven

and a fourth was at the Falcon in 1813. Principally founded to provide financial security, the social aspect of drawing together members from the local community was an important feature of their existence.

COMMUNICATIONS
Natural routes through the parish were principally east–west; the Battersea ferry and subsequent bridge, offering a limited north-south route. The Wandsworth Road/Lavender Hill, route described as the road to Kingston on the 1762 map, provided a high road, while what was to become Nine Elms Lane/Battersea Park Road, was termed the low road. The latter forked at Cross Road Shot (within today's Battersea Park) to provide a way into the village, along the subsequently named Surrey Lane.

The construction of the London & Southampton railway line after 1834 created a new means to enter or leave the parish and the terminus at Nine Elms gave Battersea a building of some architectural elegance. Designed by William Tite, the elegant portico fronted on to Nine Elms Lane just short of the boundary with Lambeth.

From Village to Suburb

The period 1790-1914 was the most momentous in the history of Battersea. When it began, the parish was rural, with a village, scattered hamlets and hundreds of acres of farmland, although there was already riverside industry and a number of pre-suburban villas and mansions. The population was just over 2,000, about the same as in 1690. By the outbreak in 1914 of the Great War, Battersea was a fully-fledged London suburb, with almost 170,000 inhabitants, equivalent to many major provincial towns.

This transformation was more concentrated, however, for the population grew from 20,000 to 169,000 between 1861 and 1901, while almost 100,000 people arrived in Battersea in the 1870s and 1880s. (Since 1914, the population has declined to its current level of about 100,000). The logistics of providing decent housing for this multitude, along with the water supply, sewers, streets, shops, pubs, schools, churches, open spaces and transport facilities were formidable. Unfortunately, it is impossible in this short compass to provide more than a brief appreciation of these vast changes and their impact on Battersea and its people.

BUILDING TRENDS AND VALUES

Building, like the economy, is cyclical, with peaks and troughs related to supply and demand, and to external factors such as finance. Battersea's housing output is summarised below.

Year	New	Total
1791	---	335
1792-1800	291	626
1801-10	92	718
1811-20	111	829
1821-30	121	950
1831-40	150	1100
1841-50	854	1954
1851-5	527	2481
1856-60	712	3193
1861-5	2218	5411
1866-70	3633	9044
1871-5	2141	11185
1876-80	4796	15981
1881-5	4036	20017
1886-90	2277	20712
1891-5	3760	24472
1896-1900	1386	25858
1901-5	1077	26935
1906-10	342	27277
1911-5	227	27504

Before 1845, building was related to local factors. Battersea New Town, begun in 1786, caused

22. *Battersea Square c.1910. The village pump has been replaced with a street lamp. A costermonger is selling his wares from a street barrow. (See also ill. 123)*

23. *The High Street c.1910. Shuttleworth Road is on the left. Many of these early 19th-century shops and houses were demolished in the 1960s and 1970s.*

an upsurge in the 1790s, but such growth was not seen again until the 1840s. Suburban expansion began in earnest after 1845, with major peaks in 1849-53, 1866-9 and 1878-82. Troughs were associated with shortages of capital and the effects of overbuilding, for example during the Crimean War, and following the peak of the late-1860s.

Before 1840, most new houses were infilling or accretions around existing settlements, notably the Village. The vast majority of new dwellings were in two/three-storied terraces, on plots 15-20ft wide by 60-100ft on green-field estates. The principal differences between houses of the 1790s and 1890s are size – two more living rooms on average in the latter – and style, although significant stylistic changes only began in the 1870s as new features filtered down to mass housing. In 1839, 70% of all Battersea houses were rented for less than £20 p.a., and by 1861, another 1,620, £11-£20 houses had been built. Of more than 6,000 houses built during the 1860s, two-thirds had rentals below £30. The basic trend in Battersea after 1840 was towards an increasingly homogeneous housing stock, leavened by parades of shops, new public houses and odd pockets of higher-value property.

The prospect of rapid financial gain was a key factor inducing landowners to exploit their estates, and with much justification. Between 1840 and 1900 land values increased by about 2,000%, ground rentals by 100% and house prices by 167%, during a period when general prices fell by 11%. Farmland grew in value from £90-150 per acre in 1835 to £2,300 in the 1860s.

Many developers used covenants in their leases to maximise the value of their estates and maintain status, with fixed rentals and with stipulated building prices for each plot. High ground rents did not always mean high status. Park Town and Wayford Street pitched high and ended up crowded with artisans; Orville Road became a slum within five years.

Most house purchases were for investment, with the houses continuing to be rented. Investors were many and varied, including gentlemen, clergymen, tradesmen and the legendary spinsters of independent means.

THE BUILDERS OF BATTERSEA 1840-1914
The creation of the suburb was the result of ant-like activity by thousands of largely ephemeral individuals working on a small scale, although the known and often considerable risks of specu-

lative building never deterred new recruits. Of the 1,423 individuals or firms who built 24,351 dwellings in Victorian Battersea, two-thirds erected ten houses or less, many only one or two. Seven-tenths worked locally in two years or less before vanishing from the record. The 7% who built more than fifty houses, were vital for the creation of the suburb, accounting for half of all houses. Most builders lived in Battersea and adjacent parishes when working locally.

Only 39 builders erected more than one hundred dwellings, accounting for one-third of the total. Thomas Penny built 768 houses at Shaftesbury Park in 1874-6. He was a front name for direct labour work by the Artizans' and General Labourers' Dwellings Co. Second was Henry Johnson who built 485 flats in mansion blocks round Battersea Park (1893-1902). Battersea Borough Council built more than 200 maisonettes at Latchmere after 1902.

Unfortunately, we have little biographical detail for this multitude of builders (Alfred Heaver is considered below). Samuel and Edwin Lathey (b. 1819 and 1832) came from Berwick St. John in Wiltshire to Battersea Fields in 1851. They were carpenters who turned to housebuilding in 1859, when they purchased land planted with cabbages and spinach on which 1-4 St. George's Road were built, at a cost of £832. The Latheys built a further 43 houses by 1867, ranging from small cottages in Aegis Grove to substantial villas in Park Road, New Wandsworth, together with parochial schools in Chatham Street and St George's vicarage. After 1870 they concentrated on work for the London School Board and the Metropolitan Police. Both brothers became local vestrymen. Edwin died in 1907, and domestic problems led to bankruptcy in 1910 and the end of a fifty-year enterprise.

With an often precarious cash-flow, many builders mortgaged houses within a few days of being granted a lease. Such mortgages averaged £150, with 5% the normal rate of interest. Building societies, 'gentlemen' and others of independent means were among those who channelled savings into bricks and mortar. Societies usually lent on the basis of the number of shares held, and were a device for funding the building of houses, not their purchase by owner-occupiers. The Reliance Permanent Benefit Building Society, founded in 1851, was associated with Battersea Baptist Chapel. By 1855 money had been advanced on 66 houses in Battersea and elsewhere. Architect William Pocock advanced bricks and

materials to builders on his Falcon Lane estate at 5%, making handsome returns. Another source of money was the sale of completed houses and of ground rents. Henry and Robert Gadd raised £2,470 on 19 houses in 1872, while Alfred Heaver sold 355 houses to the Prudential for £102,180 between 1886 and 1894.

The cyclical nature of building meant that the risk of financial disaster was ever-present. The *South London Press* reported 37 local bankruptcies 1865-70. Some builders were over-ambitious. Thomas Downard applied to build 22 houses in 1868 but was bankrupt in March the following year, while George Reeve of Camberwell, builder of 84 houses near Clapham Junction 1866-68, went out of business in January 1870. Defaulting on mortgages was often a prime cause.

Between 1851 and 1891, local employment in building increased from 359 to 6,343, supporting nearly 20% of the population by the latter date. Five major trades predominated: bricklayers, carpenters, masons, painters and plasterers, although the number of separate trades grew from 37 to 156 over the period. The rise of gasfitters from nil to 137 reflects the spread of gas for lighting and cooking. The increasing amount and complexity of sanitary fitments as water supply improved saw plumbers and allied trades grow from five to 466.

By 1887 building construction was the largest employer in Battersea. Building workers were better paid than average, but they occupied a low position in the labour hierarchy, high earnings being offset by seasonal and cyclical unemployment. Average earnings were about 33/- per week, of which 7/- went on rent, leaving just £1/6/- for food, clothing, light and other expenditure. In Charles Booth's 1890 survey the building trades account for 16% of the population. Although 73% earned average wages, Booth underscores their irregularity, with almost a quarter of building workers affected, compared with 15% overall.

Some bricks were made locally. Pocock's brickfield operated from 1845 until *c.*1882, employing nine brickmakers in 1851. William Morrison operated a small brickfield off Bridge Road, to supply his estate from 1845, and John Alder had another at the same time north of Battersea Park Road, where John Bailey agreed to pay £196 p.a. in 1846, and to make at least three million bricks, paying a royalty of 4/- per thousand. In 1884 Battersea had three brick merchants, drawing supplies from north Kent and Bedfordshire. The tiled grates and stained glass which

24. *Battersea Park Road c.1912. On the left is the General Havelock and the Cricketers public houses. The chimney served Spiers and Pond Laundry.*

grace many a late-Victorian house, came in a wide variety of styles, used to make each ostensibly identical terraced house seem different to prospective tenants.

BUILDING ESTATES IN BATTERSEA 1790-1914

The large number of estates in Victorian Battersea makes it impossible to offer more than a few brief case studies, which it is hoped may whet the reader's appetite to discover more.

Almost all new building was on 209 green-field 'estates', with 25,700 dwellings on 1,070 acres, about half the parish total. (The Thames, open spaces, industry and railways occupy 1,000 acres, the remainder being built-up by 1780.) The Crown's Battersea Park estate was created in 1846-53, while the Archbishop of York's 63 acres, built up since medieval times, was scattered across north Battersea. The largest housing developments were Crown/Battersea Park (1,552, of which 900 were flats), Park Town (1,346) and Shaftesbury Park (1,217).

One quarter of building estates predate 1850, most of them small. The 1860s were the peak period for new starts: 63 estates (31%), with 7,357 houses (29%). The period 1861-80 accounts for more than half the area and houses. After 1880 many estates replaced villas and mansions built

after 1760 around Clapham Common and along Lavender Hill. In the absence of large landowners, Battersea developments were small, averaging only five acres and 123 houses. These averages conceal wide variations, however: two-fifths had fifty houses or less, with only 9% of houses, one quarter had 51-100 houses (14%), but the 11% with 250+ houses accounted for 50% of the total.

The large number of very small estates in part reflects the late enclosure of the Common Field furlongs and strips. In 1839, 165 landowners held 1,742 acres, but only two had more than one hundred acres. The ten largest owned about one third of the parish (830 acres), while one hundred had less than five acres apiece. Many building estates were created on quarter- or half-acre strips.

There were ten major types of developers of estates, sometimes occurring in combination. Many who were described as 'gentlemen' and 'esquires' probably had an unrecorded profession or trade. Old Battersea landowners played an insignificant role, with only sixteen estates and 1,500 houses. Most owners in 1839 had sold up long before development, because of changed circumstances, failure to forecast the future, or an all-too-accurate perception of it. Most incomers bought land solely for development, and 85% of them were absentees. They account for 37 estates and 4,300 houses. Architects/surveyors (18 estates; 1,500 houses) may not have been significant

25. *Houses in Park Grove, 16 August 1956, shortly before demolition. No. 3, on the left, had already been taken down and no. 5 was soon to follow.*

developers, but builders were much more so (39 estates; 3,900 houses). Most of their creations were small estates because of the difficulty of raising capital for land purchase and building. The legal professions, involved in virtually every transaction during development, only initiated eight estates with 1,200 houses.

Other trades and professions, more prominent before 1840, were responsible for 53 estates with 5,100 houses. Again, few were local men. Examples include John Trott, ironmonger; George Bishopp and Samuel Poupart jun., both licensed victuallers. Henry Townsend, a Clapham surgeon, had two strongly contrasted estates: Lavender Hill, with substantial middle-class terraces, and Britannia Place at the bottom of the social scale. Local farmers and market gardeners sometimes cashed-in on the process, notably in northeast and north-west Battersea, for example the Carter and Gaines families.

Municipal housing began only after 1890, and the first large scheme was by the new Borough Council on Latchmere Allotments in 1903. Land and dwellings companies were much more important (12 estates; 3,250 dwellings). The Conservative Land Society and the Artizans' & General Labourers' Dwellings Co. were the most notable, with 2,130 houses. These estates tended to be built to lower densities, often on the fringes

of Battersea. Several estates were developed by a partnership of Thomas Ingram, a Brixton builder, John Brown, a Dulwich timber merchant and Henry Bragg, a Brixton gentleman. Henry Corsellis, gentleman and Arthur Corsellis, a solicitor and key figure in local administration, worked together on several estates.

The basic method of transforming fields into streets was very similar regardless of the developer or date. The use of long (90-99 year) leases and a myriad of small builders operating on often slender finances, frequently with many intermediaries between landowner and eventual occupier, was well-established before 1800, and remained the same in 1915. The capital market was fragmented, and renting was the ubiquitous form of tenure. Shaftesbury Park, where artisan owner-occupation was encouraged, was a rare exception. Progress from the initial decision to completion was very variable and often lasted decades, even on quite modest estates. Many an owner, developer and builder soon discovered that they had misread the signs and started with over-optimistic aspirations. Building could last through several ups and downs of the construction cycle, long enough to see changes of owner, layout and house type. Although half the estates were completed within five years, a quarter took more than a decade.

THE COBB ESTATE: TWELVE ACRES TO 'LITTLE HELL'

This estate lay between the Thames and the road from the village to the ferry/bridge, east of the manor house. The land was acquired by Earl Spencer in 1779, and in 1782 the Twelve Acres and Shoulder of Mutton Field were leased to Thomas Rhodes and David Meredith for 88 years. Small parcels were then let, not for riverside villas, but for industry, for example to a chemist, a soapmaker, and to James Chabot, a refiner, who subleased to Hodgson & Co., builders of the famous Horizontal Mill. The chemical works were precursors of the Morgan Crucible Co., which arrived in 1856.

Thomas Rhodes's daughter Ann married Timothy Cobb, a Banbury banker, but they were not very active in exploiting their estate. By 1809, only ten houses had appeared, mostly for factory owners and managers. In 1823 there were sixty, mostly small cottages, including Ford's Folly and Cottage Place. Shoulder of Mutton Field was still a market garden, and in 1839 the bulk of the Twelve Acres was still vacant. The deaths of Ann (1836) and Timothy Cobb (1839) were the catalyst for more rapid development. Church Road was at last diverted to run directly to Bridge Road, leaving the Folly area isolated to become a classic slum, 'Little Hell'.

An auction was held in June 1841. Joseph Watson of Chelsea was the largest purchaser. He leased many plots to John Collett, a Chelsea builder, who built the Europa beerhouse and seven houses in Church Road, later becoming the licensee there. He died in October 1852, when his estate totalled £3,309. Europa Place was worth £936, but his 34 four-room tenements in Little Europa Place were valued at only £1,105.

Bridge Road, Bridge Road West and Bolingbroke Road were all rapidly built in the 1840s boom: 170 houses were added to the existing 85 by 1851, 100 of them in 1845-6. Nos. 2-4 Westbridge Road, are two of the most unusual houses in Victorian Battersea, with flint facades and niches occupied by statues of kings. Twenty-five houses were added in Little Europa Place, and the final tally was 285. In 1851 the estate population was 1,350, and in 1861, 1,605. There was a wide social gulf between the villas of Westbridge Road and the tiny cottages in courts and alleys off Church Road. Unusually, the central area remained vacant until used for a Board School in the 1870s. Riverside industry included Howells timber yards, the Citizen Steamboat Company's yard, Edward Watson's sawmills, and May & Baker's chemical works.

In 1890, Church Road, was said to "wind considerably and from a private residential street becomes one of busy trade. The enormous plant of the Morgan Crucible Co, banks onto the river and is flanked with engineers' yards, manufacturing chemists, the Condy's Fluid manufactory, maltsters and millers. Behind the parish wharf is a very poor neighbourhood, dirty and with poor houses, known as Europa Place and Folly Lane. Bridge Rd. West, with a respectable class of house, cuts through a neighbourhood of poor streets". Europa Place, once called 'Little Hell', improved with the coming of the police and the Board School, whose log books confirm the problems with their accounts of ill-health, absenteeism, bad language and violence.

THE CROWN ESTATE AT BATTERSEA PARK

The Commissioners of Woods & Forests took virtually no advantage of the 1860s' housing boom, and the street plan of this estate was not finalised until the 1880s. New streets were approved piecemeal between 1878 and 1893 and after 1890 the vacant land was covered by blocks of mansion flats, and non-residential buildings such as Battersea Polytechnic. Not until sixty years after the 1846 Act was the estate complete.

The earliest development came in 1873, when Captain Augustus Williamson leased a large block off Albert Bridge Road. Architect John Robinson prepared a plan for 161 houses including Anhalt and Rosenau Roads (approved 1878) and work finally began in 1882-3. Thomas Wood and William Iles of Battersea built many of the houses. Despite the prestige of the estate and the large plots, Williamson granted some leases at virtually nominal rents of £2-3 p.a. Thomas Pink's, Kersley and Foxmore Streets and Kersley Mews of 1879-80 were a service area, and the Mews soon became a cab yard. Alfred Boon, a local builder-turned-developer, started in 1885 with 58 plots in the topically named Soudan and Kassala Roads. Macduff and Cupar Roads were developed by Boon on part of the Albert Palace site in 1893. Many plots were leased with a notional start in 1871, suggesting that the Crown had planned to start building just as the building cycle reached its low point.

Charles Bogue and Samuel Allin, joinery and moulding manufacturers at Nine Elms, devel-

26. *Warriner Gardens c.1910.*

27. *Emulating the large mansions to the south of Battersea Park in Prince of Wales Drive, was Albany Mansions on Albert Bridge Road, to the west of the Park, c.1910.*

oped Meath Street, although the approval was in the name of builders Lloyd & Co. In November 1878, it was reported that Lloyds had bought ten acres on which £500-800 houses were to be built, removing the "barren aspect of a large tract parallel with Battersea Park" (including Warriner Gardens).

An unusual departure was the erection of Victoria Dwellings in Battersea Park Road in 1877, three tenement blocks in a suitably forbidding style by Charles Barry junior for the Metropolitan Artizans' & Labourers' Dwelling Company. The 188 flats were subject to the usual restrictions and rules of so-called 'five percent philanthropy' companies, and were inhabited by the upper echelons of the working-class, rather than the very poor. In 1882 many of the inhabitants were skilled manual workers or employed in the transport sector.

Between 1893 and 1902, 950 mansion flats were erected, mostly along Prince of Wales Road, an impressive achievement representing almost 4% of new dwellings erected between 1780 and 1914, and more typical of Kensington than Battersea. Walter Johnson of Wood Green built about 500 flats, making him Battersea's second largest builder. The proximity of the park and river were key factors, as was the chance to make much more per acre in terms of rents and densities. The slightly Bohemian and godless image of flats and their inhabitants was noted by Booth.

THE POCOCK ESTATE

William Wilmer Pocock (1813-1899), architect, developer, Methodist lay preacher, Liberal and one-time Master of the Carpenters' Company, wrote an autobiography for his children and grandchildren. Born at Knightsbridge, he was the son of architect William Fuller Pocock and took one of the first degrees at King's College London in 1833. Choosing his father's profession in preference to the Church, Pocock joined the newly founded RIBA in 1834, becoming ARIBA in 1837 and FRIBA in 1846.

In 1840 he married Sophia Archbutt, daughter of a substantial builder. In 1855 he was a member of St. Margaret's Westminster Vestry, and of Westminster District Board of Works. In 1880 he became a Wandsworth vestryman and served two terms on the Wandsworth Board, although he did not attend regularly. Between 1879 and 1881 Pocock served as an Overseer of the Poor in Wandsworth. He stood as a Liberal for Guildford in 1865, desirous of seeing more Wesleyans in Parliament. He came third, opposed by the Tories and the clergy. Losing again at the 1866 by-election, he gave up this aspiration.

In the early 1870s, Pocock moved to The Lawn, East Hill where the adjacent ground had already been bought by a freehold land company. However, Pocock purchased the offending plots for £1,500 and then obtained the freehold for £4,000 in 1872-3. The Lawn was sold in 1886 to Henry Corsellis for £10,000, and promptly developed. Pocock died at Tunbridge Wells on 18 September 1899, and is buried in Wandsworth Cemetery.

Pocock's involvement in Battersea began in 1844, when his father bought land east of Falcon Lane containing brick-earth, and they agreed to divide the proceeds. He acquired the field in 1849 when his father died. His income was then about £1,000 p.a., mostly from leasehold houses subject to mortgages. It did not take Pocock long to realise the potential for erecting houses once the brick-earth had been removed. In March 1852, he took two plots in Falcon Grove from local market gardener Thomas Carter and purchased a further 7¾ acres at £330 an acre.

In 1852 large sheds were built for making Roberts' hollow bricks under licence. Unfortunately, the clay was not good enough, although some of the bricks were used in Prince Albert's model cottages at Windsor. Bricks were made until the late 1870s, and Pocock estimated that in thirty years he had cleared not less than £500 p.a. profit, with only one or two hours attention a week. Seventeen men were employed there in 1861, but only six in 1871 and 1881.

In 1860 the West London Extension Railway compulsorily purchased 3½ acres for £4,600, four times what Pocock had paid. This left him with most of the land and "put £1,000-1,500 in my pocket". Another £800 came from selling half-an-acre for Christchurch schools. Some land was let for building at £120 an acre p.a. in streets such as Falcon Grove and Grove (Este) Road. In 1878 Pocock purchased a strip along Guildford Street for £500 to provide sufficient depth to build houses, once the road had been realigned. In 1882 the School Board paid £2,362 for the site of Shillington Street School. By Christmas 1882 Pocock was making £128 p.a. from ground rents, pushing the value of the land to at least £2,500. He advanced money and bricks to builders and charged 5%. In doing so he cleared £30-40,000 from the Falcon Brickfield during its life. His remark "in helping others I helped myself" needs no comment.

Pocock's 285-house estate took more than thirty years and three building peaks to complete. There were only 52 houses by 1861. The five years from 1876 were the most productive, with 100 new houses. Pocock favoured 75/80-year terms with ground rents on the low side at about 5/- per foot. Despite his influence on the first middle-class houses in Falcon Road and Falcon Grove, the design of most was severely plain, owing more to the speculative builders' ideas of what would let. Booth classified most of the Pocock Estate as poverty and comfort mixed (D), and Duffield Street somewhat surprisingly as E (average earnings). The houses and shops along Falcon Road were lower middle-class.

ALFRED HEAVER

Alfred Heaver (1841-1901) made a significant impact not only in Battersea, but across a wide swathe of south-west London. Born in Lambeth on 10 February 1841, he was the fourth child of George Heaver, carpenter (1814-92). Nothing in his origins or early life suggests that Alfred would do other than follow in his father's footsteps. In 1863, described as a carpenter, he married Isabella Luetchford, a baker's daughter. When she died in 1874 Heaver married her younger sister Patience, when he was described as a builder.

Patience died in 1887, and Heaver, by now a contractor, married Fanny Tutt from Oxfordshire. He had eight children (two sons and six daughters). Heaver was murdered by his brother-in-law on his way to church from his country house at Westcott, Dorking in August 1901: a hundred employees were said to have attended his funeral. Heaver appeared in Battersea in 1869 in partnership with Edward Coates (born Lambeth 1845), an association that lasted until Heaver's death. Until 1878, Heaver remained a small-scale builder, with around forty houses to his name (about five per year). Thereafter, however, he began to buy land for development, and for the rest of the century was a significant initiator of estates, not only in Battersea, but also in Fulham, Balham and Tooting, as well as building many houses. The reason for this sudden change is unknown.

He was elected to the District Board in 1879. The scale of his operations progressively increased, with new estates being developed almost annually from 1879, totalling 4,000 houses, of which six, with 1,160 houses, including many shops, were in Battersea. His best-known development is the 1,250-house Heaver Estate in Balham, started in 1888.

Heaver and Coates built at least 730 houses, including 530 in Balham and Tooting in the 1890s.

28.   Belleville Road, c.1910.

Ground rents alone would have made Heaver wealthy, but he did not retain them long, selling off blocks of property to finance new land purchases, street and sewer construction. The Prudential Assurance Company bought from him 355 houses / shops in central Battersea for £102,000 between 1886 and 1894. Heaver's estate when he died in 1901 was valued in excess of £625,000, about £35m. at today's prices. The similar style of the houses on many Heaver estates probably reflects his ideas, together with those of his surveyors / architects.

His first development was the extension of Belleville and Wakehurst Roads from Northcote Road to Webbs Road. The plans were by William Poole, whom Heaver was to employ many times. The semi-detached houses had generous 20-21ft. plots, giving Heaver £420 p.a. from ground rents, hardly sufficient to enable him to embark on his next, much larger scheme. Falcon Park, nineteen acres astride Falcon Road, was laid out by Poole and approved in May 1879. Several street-names commemorated the current Afghan War, but the politically incorrect Zulu Crescent soon became Rowena. In March 1879 Edward Fownes of the glove-making family agreed with Heaver to grant 99-year leases. Phase 1 comprised 178 lots, Phase 2, 234 lots and Phase 3, 62. Houses were to be worth at least £250 (£350 in Falcon Road and

facing Christchurch). The junction of Patience and Khyber Roads was earmarked for a £700 hotel, but this was never built, and neither was the projected vestry hall at the junction of Falcon and Battersea Park Roads. Before building began, some land was used for fêtes and sports. Poplar House was demolished in late 1880 and forty builders covered this last vacant land north of Clapham Junction with great speed. In 1879, 174 houses were built in eight months, followed by 375 in 1880 – seven per week. The principal builders were John Jenkins (53 houses), Heaver (49), William Rowe (42), Edward Nixon (38) and Daniel Pitt (33).

Heaver purchased the Chatto Estate off Clapham Common in 1880-1 and Poole drew up plans for 'Heaver Park'. These were never approved and the estate was resold. Perhaps Heaver had over-reached, although he immediately proceeded with the Dives Estate (Lavender Sweep), the property of Thomas Dives, owner of Church Road flour mill. Poole produced the plans in April 1881. The estate had long frontages to Lavender Hill and St John's Road, both lined with substantial terraces of shops, the first stage in transforming a hitherto rural area into the new commercial centre of Battersea. The corner site was occupied by Messrs Arding & Hobbs department store, although it too had been canvassed

29. Northcote Road, c.1907. Several costermongers have their carts and stalls set out on the west side of the road.

30. Lavender Sweep, c.1910.

as suitable for the new vestry hall. Progress was slower here, eight builders taking until 1884 to complete 146 houses/shops. Thomas Spearing and John Rowe each built 40, about half with shops. Frederick Bailey built a block of 24 fronting Lavender Sweep and Beauchamp Road.

In August 1885 Charles Bentley, a Wandsworth architect, submitted plans for the Shrubbery Estate. The mansion it contained (i.e. The Shrubbery) survived, having been acquired by Canon Erskine Clarke, Vicar of Battersea for use as a school. St Barnabas church was built in front of it in 1898. The 52 houses in Lavender Gardens are very large, albeit terraced, and rapidly completed in 1887-8. They were in the same style as those on the Dives Estate, with prominent dog's-tooth moulding above the ground floor, common on Heaver's estates, but also widespread in south and south-west London 1875-90.

Heaver's next venture, also planned by Bentley, was approved in April 1886. St John's Park contained 225 houses, including parades of shops along the west side of St John's Road and in St John's Hill. Most of the land belonged to Matthew Whiting, who continued to live at Lavender Lodge opposite, entirely surrounded by Heaver's estates until his death in 1903. St John's Park was rapidly finished. John Rowe built 68 houses,

31. St John's Road c.1890. The photograph shows single storey shops built in 1889 in front of Whynot Villas, which date from c.1845.

32. Lavender Gardens, c.1910.

including 28 shops, and A. Bennett 43. In December 1887, Heaver was about to embark on his most ambitious project in Balham, and sold a large part of St John's Park to the Prudential for £29,700.

Heaver's final Battersea development was the Chestnuts estate on the north side of Lavender Hill. It had been the home of Mrs Stirling, an actress, and the core of her house still stands at 22-28 Mossbury Road. Bentley's plans were approved in April 1887 and all but two of the 87 houses and shops were built that year, a sure indication of how well Heaver had created a market round Clapham Junction. All 31 shops on Lavender Hill and Falcon Road were built by Thomas & Co. of Gunnersbury. Leases ranged from £6 p.a. up to £28 for a prime corner shop site.

Including Kambala Road, where he was the joint developer, Alfred Heaver provided houses for upwards of 8,000 people in Battersea, putting a distinctive stamp on large areas. In addition, 175 shops were provided, mostly at Clapham Junction and in Falcon Road, making him the largest retail developer in the suburb. In total, the property on his estates would have produced ground rents in excess of £9,500 p.a., and the capital value of the buildings was at least £400,000. Many of the estates were located on the suburban frontier of the time, the sale particulars stressing the proximity of railways and tramways. Most of the Battersea estates were within ten minutes' walk of Clapham Junction and on tram routes.

Falcon Park was typical of north Battersea, the home of skilled workers, clerks and small shopkeepers, with 70% employed in building, manufacture and transport, the majority of them locally. Other estates, south of the railway, had 70-80% of households belonging to the lower-middle classes, with up to 40% in the retail/distribution sector. Booth's view of all these estates was "fairly comfortable", with the retail fringes "wealthy". Only Musjid Road, where there was an element of poverty, and Lavender Gardens, all middle-class, diverged from the norm.

33. *Sabine Road on the Shaftesbury Park Estate c.1908.*

SOME CONTEMPORARY VIEWS OF DEVELOPMENT

The *South London Press*, which began in 1865, provides valuable evidence for the mushroom growth of Battersea. In October 1866, it reported "a large town of shops and dwellings on what was once Battersea Fields from Nine Elms to York Road. Although only three years old, extensive additions are being made to the [Clapham] Junction station, around which builders are hard at work".

In October 1869 as the building cycle turned rapidly down, 'A Tradesman' wrote about the distressed state of Battersea, caused by high rents. "In the old days when houses were not rabbit hutches, and not built on the Japanese plan, of paper, 8% was a reasonable return on outlay. Now, with fictitiously large ground rents, ingenious surveyors and grasping lawyers, the poor hard-working good-natured speculative builder has to swallow his conscience and his figures." He claimed that there were "one thousand empty houses in Battersea eating themselves up with ground rents, as well as becoming dilapidated". (There were 1,345 empty houses in 1871, and 435 under construction.) The builder, often the object

of criticism, had plenty of potential scapegoats among greedy landowners, financiers and lawyers. A few weeks later, however, 'Another Tradesman' commented that "in the Queen's Road extension and adjacent streets [Park Town], superior house property which has been empty for years because of high rents is now letting at one-half to two-thirds of the previous rents".

In 1870 'A Blighted Suburb – New Battersea' was said to be a "neglected area, despite the railways and the park [and] has brought many builders to bankruptcy. Some have seriously considered pulling down their property for the sake of the bricks and timber". Meetings had been held with a view to getting Battersea populated, and "in some cases policemen, wharfingers, labourers and their families with only enough to fill one or two rooms are the sole inhabitants of six-eight roomed houses". Tolls on Chelsea Bridge could cost a family up to 2/- per week and freeing it would "greatly entice people from over the water". (This happened in 1879.) "The expression 'Go to Battersea' has arisen as one of general contempt." All kinds of inducements were being offered to lure tenants, such as free rent for the first month and then 7/- p.w. for an eight-room

34. Tennyson Street c.1911. The children are heading for Tennyson Street school, which is on the right.

house at a time when 4s 6d - 5s was a common rent for only 2-3 rooms.

A few years later over-supply was again a threat, and builders who, "in view of [the new] Queen's Road station [opened 1877] and freeing of the bridges [1879] have run up tenements, have not found them filling quickly because of high rents of 15-16/- per week for six-roomed houses". A correspondent complained of the poor service at the new station (still the case 125 years later), suggesting that a board with the words 'wanted, trains' be put up!

In 1877, the Vicar of St. Peter's, complained that houses built "on rubbish and dust shoots, without basements and with boarded floors close to the earth", caused much local sickness. Henry Hansom, District Surveyor for north Battersea, cast grave doubts on suburban building.

"Speculative builders appear, a creation or organism unknown to science or art, the outcome of the growth of London and the compulsory [sic] removal of the working classes to the suburbs in such large numbers. Architects for houses disappear, estates have to be floated, frequently by capitalists or financial agents distinct from the freeholder. [The] sole object is a quick return. The speculative builder is often no builder at all, but a bricklayer, carpenter, labourer, mechanic, tradesman, butler or retired policeman, even clergymen."

A damning indictment, although in fairness, the quality of most Battersea houses was not too bad.

Victorian Society

WORKING LIVES

Victorian Battersea was *par excellence* a suburb of the skilled working class, which accounted for 42% of households in 1851 (*c*.2,000 people) to 56% in 1871 and 61% in 1881-91, equivalent to 93,000 people at the latter date. The non-manual element (for example, clerks, shop assistants, railwaymen of various types) within this group declined from 43% in 1851 to 33% in 1871, reflecting the rapid growth of industry and building work. Thereafter, it increased rapidly once more to reach 48% in 1891, with many newcomers working in the service sector, both locally, where the number of shops had grown rapidly, and in London.

As Battersea was transformed from a large village to a working-class suburb, the proportion of upper- and middle-class households declined from 6% in 1851 to around 1.5% for the rest of the century – the unfulfilled proposal to build Regent's Park-like villas and terraces around Battersea Park would have helped to maintain this element. The lower middle-class, including retailers and some professionals as well as employers of labour, maintained its importance until 1871 with 16-19% of the population. Thereafter, the attractions of Battersea paled compared with suburbs such as Wandsworth and Streatham, and this element fell to around 10% of households, although this still represents around 16,000 people in 1891, compared with about 9-10,000 in 1871.

Semi-skilled workers accounted for 12-15% of households. Parts of north Battersea were noted for concentrations of laundry workers and charwomen, both key employments for female heads of household. Many semi-skilled men worked in the gasworks and other local industries. The proportion of unskilled labour declined from 20% in 1851-61 to 10% in 1891. Many were labourers in riverside factories, building and transport, often seasonal work prone to unemployment.

Agriculture had ceased to be a major employer by 1851, although the growing army of horses for passenger and freight transport caused a slight increase after 1881. Employment in the building industry grew rapidly from 10% of household heads in 1851 to 19% in 1871-81, before falling to 13% in 1901 as the suburb was completed. The retail and distribution sector grew from 10 to 14% as new shops and pubs were provided, as well as associated wholesale requirements. Domestic service includes not only servants, but also trades such as laundering. This sector halved in importance 1851-91, from 15 to 7%, although this still represents 10,500 people, the same as the total population forty years earlier.

Manufacturing, from gas-making, building railway locomotives and chemicals to domestic shoemaking and tailoring, remained remarkably constant at 26-28% of the total (about 40,000 people depended on this sector in 1891). People with private means were never significant (2-5% of households), and although the economic impact of the very wealthy was considerable, many were relatively poor, for example widows living on a few house rents. Public sector and professional employment grew in line with the total population, with around 8-9% of the total. Employment in transport grew progressively from 7% in the early days of the suburb to 11%, the fourth largest group. Railways took the lion's share, although in earlier decades river work was important, and trams played a part from 1880.

CHARLES BOOTH'S SURVEY

Charles Booth's survey of 1889 divided society into eight classes based on earnings. Class A, the Lowest/Semi-Criminal, was estimated at 714 individuals in Battersea (0.5%; shown in black on Booth's famous Poverty Map). They were mainly concentrated in Nine Elms, cut off from the outside world by gasworks and railways. Class B (Casual Earnings, dark blue) contained 7,737 (5%), and Class C, (Irregular Earnings light blue), some 22,856 (15%). These three classes represent the unskilled and semi-skilled, and occur in pockets across north Battersea. With Class D (Regular Minimum Earnings, purple), we move into the lower echelons of the skilled working class. There were 19,783 people in this group (13%). Class E, (Standard Earnings, pink) with 58,718 individuals (38%) is the quintessential Battersea of the late-Victorian period, skilled workmen in manufacturing and transport, and the burgeoning army of clerks, shop workers and many domestic servants. Class F, (Highly Paid Artisans, red) 28,420 people (19%) are the local labour aristocracy, earning in excess of 40/- per week. Classes G (Lower Middle Class, 11,593 [7.5%] and H (Middle Class, 3,064 [2%], both yellow), although only a small proportion, were significant numbers making a considerable impact on the local economy. Almost all 'yellow' streets were in central and south Battersea.

LODGERS

In the Victorian period, about half of Battersea household heads were born in Surrey and Middlesex, with around 20% each from the other Home Counties and the rest of England. With the exception of Irish-born heads in 1871, the rest of the United Kingdom provided very few migrants. The transformation of village to suburb led to a halving of the numbers born in Battersea, from 10 to 5%.

In 1881 and 1891 one-sixth of Battersea families took in either lodgers or boarders. Lodgers were concentrated in the Village area and in the streets south of Battersea Park Road, while boarders were mostly in New Town. Both were much less significant in skilled working class and clerks'/ shopworkers' areas, where the pressure on family finances was reduced by regular earnings. Servant-keeping was less unusual than might be expected, 7-8% of families having living-in servants, with many more having daily help. Servant-keeping was a feature of New Wandsworth, Lavender Hill and south Battersea generally, and was conspicuous by its absence north of the LSWR.

Straightforward lodging houses were uncommon in Battersea. There were six in 1891, all close to the old Village. No.111 Westbridge Road housed 43 men, including 32 labourers and six building workers. More than fifty men were crowded into 116-120 High Street, but the census unusually omits any details for individuals. Lodging houses at 37-41 and 65-67 Surrey Lane housed 56 and 29 men. None of these premises was large or purpose-built, so the overcrowding and living conditions are difficult to imagine.

WAGES

According to a Board of Trade survey in 1887, average earnings in Battersea were about 30/- per week, about the level of the higher-paid artisan. However, 19% were unemployed, of whom three-quarters had been out of work for more than three months, and another 21% were in irregular employment. Only 61% worked regularly. Overall, 20-25% of income was paid in rent, buying the use of three rooms. (In Lambeth in 1910, the poorest families spent 30% on rent, and that was probably true in Battersea.) Average family size was just over five persons, giving a density of two per room.

Despite better-than-average earnings, the standard of living in Battersea in the late-1880s does not seem to have been especially high. For every family living in relative luxury, there were many more eking out an unpleasant existence in crowded, often insanitary premises. Even with supplementary earnings from wives, children, lodgers and boarders, many household budgets were fully-committed to rent and food, and 40% ran the risk that earnings might be irregular, or even cease altogether for months at a time.

POLARISATION

Some areas were able to maintain their status, while others declined. The area east of the Village had many high-quality houses in 1850, but by 1880 they had been swamped by the emergence of slums nearby. The Village itself remained socially mixed, a legacy from the time when it *was* Battersea. Streets off York Road, which had a concentration of skilled manual workers in 1851, had deteriorated by 1871 as they were replaced by the unskilled. 'New Wandsworth' managed to retain its middle classes status for many years. The area south of Battersea Park Road, developed 1850-1870, had a concentration of skilled manual workers in 1871, declining to semi-skilled by 1891 as the housing aged. A similar fate befell estates north of Clapham Junction, once the first flush of newness wore off. Park Town, whose grand terraces had been aimed at the middle classes, was unsuccessful, and became a colony of skilled workers in multiple occupancy. Nearby, the Shaftesbury Estate (1872-77) was similar, although here the result was intentional, with single-family houses, many of them owner-occupied.

By 1891 a strong polarisation between north and south Battersea had become apparent, divided by the LSWR embankment, not by any natural feature. To the north, Battersea Park provided the only relief in a sea of two-storey terraced houses. In the south higher ground was largely the preserve of the upper and middle classes, terrace housing having only begun to sweep across here after 1880.

In this, Battersea was a microcosm of London as a whole, its two areas almost as different as two nations. There was a stark contrast between the poverty endured by tens of thousands in north Battersea and the relative, even absolute comfort of a few in the south. The role of the Commons in maintaining social status was crucial. Had they been enclosed before about 1850, Battersea would undoubtedly have evolved very differently. Equally, Battersea Park prevented all of north Battersea disappearing under a tide of houses, factories and railways, although it was a close run thing since development had begun to stir there in the 1840s. However, in many streets the degree of social mixing was considerable, belying the superficial similarity of the housing types. The upper classes, rare in Battersea after 1850, appear to have preserved pockets of exclusivity, notably around the Commons, although their continued presence in the old Village close to some of the worst slums emphasises the fact that segregation was not always the norm.

Contemporary descriptions help to flesh out the dry statistics and provide glimpses of life in late-Victorian Battersea. It was atypical in certain respects, "combining industries of its own by the river with the most perfect specimen of a working-class residential district in the Shaftesbury Estate. The aspect to travellers, north of Clapham Junction, is a wilderness of houses, chiefly of two storeys, with church spires, a fringe of factory chimneys, and the conspicuous masses of the Board Schools rising high above the dead level of the roofs". Laundry work employed large numbers of women, mainly at home, although the great catering firm of Spiers & Pond had its laundry in Battersea Park Road.

By 1890, the market gardens and piggeries for which Battersea had been noted were largely a thing of the past. Gipsies wintered in their caravans locally, for example at Donovan's Yard, sandwiched between railway lines. In 1900 it housed two long lines of wagons and some firewood-sellers' huts.

Shaftesbury Park was home to "the intelligent portion of local socialism, and the colony represents the high water mark of the intelligent London artisan".

THE POOREST AREAS

At the other end of the spectrum, the worst elements took refuge in areas cut off by blank walls or railways such as Little Europa Place, hemmed-in by factories. In 1871 only seven of the 108 children there went to school. The Ponton Estate in Nine Elms, the worst slum in Battersea, was virtually cut off from the rest by railways, gas and water works. Britannia Place, Plough Lane, self-contained with poor access, Latchmere Grove, hemmed-in by two railway lines and once the location of many insanitary piggeries, Brougham and Berkley Streets off Culvert Road, another isolated estate turned in on itself, and the Linford Street area, surrounded by railway works and factories, were other real or potential slums. Although some had been built as long ago as the 1820s and 1830s, most were typical two-storey terraces built after 1860, and not necessarily jerry-

built or predestined to decline. Environment was the crucial factor, leading to progressive drift down the social scale as artisans moved out to more salubrious areas.

The Nine Elms enclave, mostly built 1860-70, had "broken windows, cracked plaster, dirty children and drink-sodden women". Barefoot, even naked, children were common, and people often slept in the streets in summer to avoid the vermin. The gasworks provided well paid, but seasonal and dangerous work, while many worked as costermongers. Orville Road was a much more recent pocket of poverty and crime. It was developed from 1884. Each house had three floors, separately occupied and with three rooms. The earliest occupants were artisans, but after a year "some bad lots got in [on] the odd-numbered side and change set in. Families with little or no furniture, continually on the move, going hopping [hop-picking] in summer". Street gamblers were common, with pickets posted at the ends of the street to warn of the police. Speke Road next to Clapham Junction contained poor three-storey houses, many "out of repair and wretchedly built; at least four windows show 'mangling done here'".

Sharp contrasts existed over short distances. Near Battersea Bridge were large cab depots, a Salvation Army salvage wharf, the Imperial Oil Company's stores, Wellington refinery, Ransome's Dock and a brass foundry, while around Battersea Park were large houses and blocks of flats, although bakeries and catering firms were colonising Battersea Park Road, soon to be followed by the Polytechnic.

Large homogeneous tracts were the exception. The Carter Estate (1840-70) was "a region of small streets, badly kept, with poor shops and a poor class of people", but nearby Harbut and Maysoule Roads "are new and well built" (1881-4). East of Plough Lane "all the roads are lined with commonplace terrace houses the roads and footways crowded with playing children". Heaver's Falcon Park estate was "better, clean and regularly built", but nearby Pocock's and other estates contained "drab little houses, generally more or less sublet to lodgers". Little Europa Place was "a very poor neighbourhood, dirty and with poor houses", while Nine Elms was "a mass of small streets at all angles inclined to squalor, overrun by children".

Battersea New Town and the area off Thessaly Road were generally better, although Linford Street and its environs were "small and mean and in places filthy; shops of the worst type ministering to poorly paid wage-earners, among them

35. Children gather outside a confectioner's shop in Webbs Road c.1910. Belleville Road school is on the left.

are evil-smelling fish bars and the inevitable small squalid public houses with their attendant secondhand dealers". The great mass of streets, off Battersea Park Road were, "small and mean, eminently squalid, some soulless being has named them after romantic kings and English premiers". (Arthur and Alfred were in fact sons of Queen Victoria). Broughton and Stanley Streets, grandiose terraces in Park Town were "shadeless and swarming with children", a far cry from the aspirations of their developers. Carpenter and Blondel Streets were "very clean", whereas most streets here were full of small, dirty houses, "the people far from cleanly, while troops of children are obliged to play in the gutters." Knots of idlers adorned each corner along the main road. Conditions within were doubtless a strong incentive to live much of life outdoors. In 1890 the only area of active building was between Lavender Hill and Clapham Common, "an entire district cut up with new roads and others in the making."

THE LOCAL SHOPS

Pre-urban Battersea possessed few shops and a scattering of traditional inns. Much of the food and commodities required by the population were no doubt produced locally, or brought from itinerant traders and even in 1840 the High Street had scarcely any shops. All this soon changed dramatically, and most new estates included purpose-built shops and additional public and beer houses. Between 1852 and 1871, the number of shops increased from 168 to 818, matching

growth in population. There were also 93 new drink outlets, although here growth was only half as fast. How much this was due to the temperance movement and the restrictions by certain estate developers and magistrates is not clear.

The characteristic parades of shops lining many main roads began to appear after 1860. Battersea Park Road and York Road were followed by Lavender Hill, Falcon Road, St John's Road and Northcote Road, the last with a street market. All this decisively moved the commercial centre of the suburb to Clapham Junction. There were also corner shops on most estates. By 1891 there were 1,656 shops and 280 drink outlets, giving 90 inhabitants per shop, and 534 for each drink outlet. By then Battersea had its own department store – Arding & Hobbs, and there were several other large stores offering a wide range of goods, some in multiple premises.

Henry Arding and Mr Hobbs founded their large department store in a small shop in Wandsworth High Street in 1876 selling drapery and house furnishings. They quickly took over a second and third shop, selling furniture. The developing area of Clapham Junction was good for business and they then took on five shops in Falcon Road, and then bought Tom Taylor's estate at the corner of Lavender Hill and St John's Road for a new store, which they opened in 1885. In 1905 Hobbs retired, leaving the firm in the hands of the Arding family.

The store, employing 400, was totally destroyed by a fire on 20 December 1909, with eight people

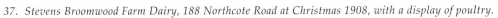

36. *Parkes Drug Stores, 313 Lavender Hill, c.1908. The telephone number was given as 543 Putney, the local exchange at the time being at Putney.*

37. *Stevens Broomwood Farm Dairy, 188 Northcote Road at Christmas 1908, with a display of poultry.*

38. H. Gardner, dealer in second-hand furniture, utensils, china and books, at 142 High Street c.1908. Second-hand dealers did good business in the High Street area.

39. Smyth, bakers and confectioners, 83 Chatham Road, at the corner of Northcote Road, c.1914.

40. *Arding and Hobbs store, shortly before the fire in December 1909.*

41. *Policemen stand guard over the ruins of the fire at Arding & Hobbs.*

losing their lives. A Christmas display of turkeys in a shop opposite was cooked by the ferocity of the blaze.

The replacement store, designed by James Gibson, was far larger than its predecessor. It opened on 6 December 1910. A merger took place in 1938 with the John Anstee Group and in 1948 the store became part of the United Drapery Stores Group. It is now within the John Alders Group.

Food shops, half the total in 1891, were vital in managing the Victorian working-class budget. The need to make repeated small purchases of items such as bread, tea and potatoes, as well as the absence of refrigeration, contributed to their proliferation. The large number of clothing and variety/general stores reflected intense competition between small shopkeepers in an age before multiple retailers.

In 1887, workers in shops had average earnings of 30/- per week (bakers 27/7d; butchers 24/-), four-fifths were in regular employment. In Booth's survey, 'Dealers' accounted for 6% of the population, shopmen and assistants for another 3%. More than 13,000 local people were dependent on retailing, of whom 20%. were "very poor or poor". Shop workers and small shopkeepers belonged mainly to Classes E/F (ordinary standard earnings/highly paid). Large shopkeepers, and most coffee and licensed house keepers were in classes F and G. Street sellers were of much lower status. Two-thirds of them had casual or irregular earnings, or regular minimum wages.

42. *The sumptuous furnishing and drapery floor of the rebuilt Arding and Hobbs, probably December 1910.*

43. *An Arding and Hobbs delivery van c.1930.*

ARDING & HOBBS, L^{TD}.

WAREHOUSING
in
SPACIOUS
MODERN
DEPOSITORIES.

MUSICAL
INSTRUMENTS
stored in
SEPARATE
HEATED ROOMS.

SPECIAL
FACILITIES
for
BAGGAGE.

REMOVALS
with
SAFETY, SPEED
and
SKILL.

We offer you a
SPECIALIZED
SERVICE with
MODERN equip-
ment & Highly-
Skilled Men.

ESTIMATES
and
ADVICE FREE.

CLAPHAM JUNCTION, S.W. 11.

44. *Building the support wall for the new Battersea Bridge c.1889.*

Bridges

THE NEW BRIDGE

Amazingly, the old wooden Battersea bridge survived until 1883, when it closed to be replaced by a temporary footbridge, while a new iron structure was built. Designed by Sir Joseph Bazalgette, chief engineer of the Metropolitan Board of Works, it was opened by Lord Rosebery, on 31 July 1890. With a width of only forty feet it is one of the narrowest in London. The old bridge had been compulsorily purchased by the Albert Bridge Company in 1873, from whom the MBW took over. Both bridges were freed from tolls in April 1879, the Prince and Princess of Wales making a series of ceremonial crossings to mark the occasion.

CHELSEA BRIDGE

Battersea acquired another Thames crossing when Chelsea Bridge was opened on 28 March 1858 – the same day as the new park. The two projects were conceived as a whole, under Acts of 1846. Among the provisions was compensation to the Watermen's Company for the loss of a Sunday ferry to the Red House, a noted place of resort on the Battersea riverside. Chelsea Bridge was a suspension bridge some seven hundred feet long, with a main span of 350 feet between two pairs of ornate towers, surmounted by large globe-shaped lamps. The iron work came from Edinburgh, and the design was by Thomas Page, architect of the second Westminster Bridge. At each end stood attractive toll houses, where foot passengers were charged ½d; the toll for horses was 2d. The bridge was freed from toll in 1879 and demolished in 1935. The present bridge was opened on 6 May 1937.

ALBERT BRIDGE

The last local road bridge was named in memory of Prince Albert, and built under an Act of 1864. The site lay at the western end of Battersea Park, surprisingly close to Battersea Bridge, although it opened up an area of Battersea for middle-class housing which had hitherto remained untouched. Work on the Chelsea Embankment delayed the start till 1870. R.M. Ordish's rigid suspension principle was used, in which the main girders carry the roadway by straight chains suspended from a steel cable. The bridge is 710 feet long and 41 feet wide and the centre span is of 400 feet. The four towers lie outside the main frame, and

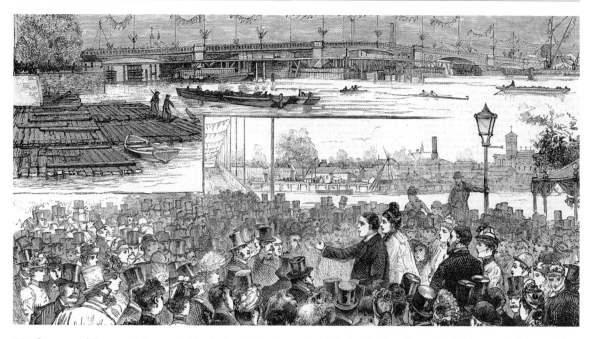

45. *Opening of the new Battersea Bridge by Lord Rosebery on 21 July 1890. The old wooden bridge was left in position while the new bridge was under construction.*

the whole structure has an airy gothic feel to it. The cylinders of the piers were cast in Battersea by Robinson & Cottam, the superstructure by Handyside of Derby and the steel cables by the Cardigan Works of Sheffield. There were four small lodges for the collection of tolls, illegal passage being prevented by two bars. Albert Bridge opened first on 31 December 1872, but was soon closed, reopening again on 23 August 1873. The cost was estimated at £90,000. The Greater London Council provided the central supports in the 1970s, saving the structure from collapse.

RAILWAY BRIDGES
By far the largest of Battersea's bridges is the Grosvenor or Victoria railway bridge, which carries the lines of the erstwhile London, Brighton & South Coast Railway and the London, Chatham Dover Railway/Great Western Railway into Victoria. The first stone of the bridge was laid on 9 June 1859, and the first train crossed on 9 June 1860. Sir John Fowler was the engineer, and the LBSCR and LCDR/GWR each put up half the cost. At first, there were only two tracks, laid with mixed standard- and broad-gauge to accommodate the GWR. Widening was soon needed, and took place under Sir Charles Fox, at the same time

as the new high-level approaches were being built on the Battersea side, in 1866. Five tracks were added, making it the widest railway bridge in the world at that time. In 1901, two more tracks were added to what were in effect three separate bridges. In its final form the Grosvenor Bridge had four 175ft. spans with wrought-iron ribs and cast-iron standards. It was rebuilt in steel between 1963 and 1968, with ten tracks, since reduced to nine.

The furthest west of Battersea's bridges was also a railway bridge, taking the West London Extension Railway from Fulham to Battersea. It is now known as Cremorne Bridge, after the pleasure grounds in Chelsea, but was at first more prosaically Battersea New Bridge or Railway Bridge. It opened in March 1863, and consists of five 120ft. spans in cast-iron, with stone piers carried up above parapet level to provide some relief. The design was by William Baker, chief engineer of the London North-Western Railway, and the cost £87,000. Part of a vital cross-Thames link, it was little used by passenger services from 1940 until the 1990s, but now carries everything from local trains to Eurostar trains en route to their North Pole depot in north Kensington. The bridge was strengthened in 1969 and again in 1992.

46. *Chelsea Bridge c.1915.*

47. *Albert Bridge c.1910.*

On the Move

Innovations in public transport, especially the railway, had a very significant impact on Battersea after 1840. Before that, those who wanted to travel had very limited opportunities even if they had the time and money to do so, although the wealthier newcomers in the villas and mansions around the two Commons could afford their own vehicles. Most people relied on river craft of various kinds, including the Chelsea ferry until 1771. Goods traffic too had gone by river, and the riverside at Battersea reflected that. Building stone from the Surrey hills was transhipped at a wharf close to the mouth of the Falcon Brook as early as the twelfth century.

By the 1820s and 1830s passenger travel was by carriers' carts and short stage and omnibus services, but these did not affect the essentially local orientation of employment. But the advent of the railway locally in 1838 brought a dramatic transformation, and by 1900 transport was the fourth largest employer in the area, with 10% of households involved.

COMING OF THE RAILWAYS

The London & Southampton Railway was built in the late 1830s, very soon after the steam locomotive had proved itself a feasible form of traction. It opened in stages from May 1838, beginning with the Nine Elms (its first London terminus) to Woking section; Southampton was reached in June 1839. The choice of a relatively remote terminus in Battersea reflected the high cost of property in central London (*cf.* the other early termini at Paddington and Euston). The line crossed the low-lying fields and marshes of Battersea on a long embankment. Bridges were provided for the few pre-existing roads and these had a marked effect on the pattern of suburban development after 1850. Beyond the site of Clapham Junction the line passed into a deep cutting through Wandsworth Common. There was a station at Battersea Rise, called Wandsworth, later renamed Clapham Common, setting a precedent for railways largely to ignore the name of Battersea. This difficult site was probably chosen because St John's Hill was still a turnpike {toll} road at that time. The London & Southampton Railway changed its name to London & South Western Railway (LSWR) in 1839.

48. Nine Elms station, dating from 1838, was found to be too far from London and was superseded when Waterloo was opened in 1848. Nine Elms then became the goods depot for the London and South-Western Railway.

49. *Heavy lifting breakdown crane at No. 1 Loco Department, Nine Elms c.1908.*

50. *A Southern Railway locomotive* **Lord Nelson** *at Longhedge/Stewarts Lane Works in 1931. In the background is Hampton & Sons depository, later in use by Decca the electrical manufacturers.*

51. *A LSWR train of four passenger carriages and a flat truck transporting a carriage, passing along the cutting near the Freemasons' Girls' School in the 1850s.*

Services began with six down and five up trains (four each way on Sundays). Fares from Wandsworth to Nine Elms were 1/6d first-class and 1s second-class for only three miles, far beyond the reach of the majority. Third-class passengers were not carried. The LSWR was not a suburban railway, the average journey in 1839 being 21 miles. In any case, there was little building in what later became the south-western suburbs of London and therefore few passengers to attract railway companies. From Nine Elms, travellers made their way to London proper by boat or cab. The line was extended to Waterloo in 1848, when Nine Elms became the principal goods depot instead. The locomotive works for the railway and its largest engine shed had been here since 1843.

In July 1846, the Richmond Railway was opened from the LSWR at Falcon Lane via Wandsworth and Putney. This was clearly intended as a suburban line, catering also for the pleasure traffic to the Thames Valley. It was worked from the start by the LSWR, which provided two additional tracks to Nine Elms and Waterloo, but no interchange station at the junction. Only six

dwellings were affected in Battersea, the rest of the area crossed being gardens, meadows or market garden ground.

Apart from its physical presence and modest employment at Nine Elms, the railway had little impact on Battersea at first and the census of 1851 shows only 64 railwaymen in the parish, of whom 56 were at Nine Elms. There were a dozen engine drivers and the rest ranged from Richard Eaton, the locomotive superintendent, to porters and labourers.

The first Railway Mania collapsed in the late 1840s, and the next local line did not open until 1856. The West End of London & Crystal Palace Railway (WECPR) connected the relocated Crystal Palace with the West End of London. (The site of the palace and its grounds lay mostly in Penge, a detached portion of Battersea parish until 1888.) The WECPR reached a temporary terminus at Battersea Rise on 1 December 1856 and was extended to 'Pimlico' station in March 1858. This was a very odd station name since it was in Battersea next to the new Park and Chelsea Bridge. The line finally reached Victoria on 1 October

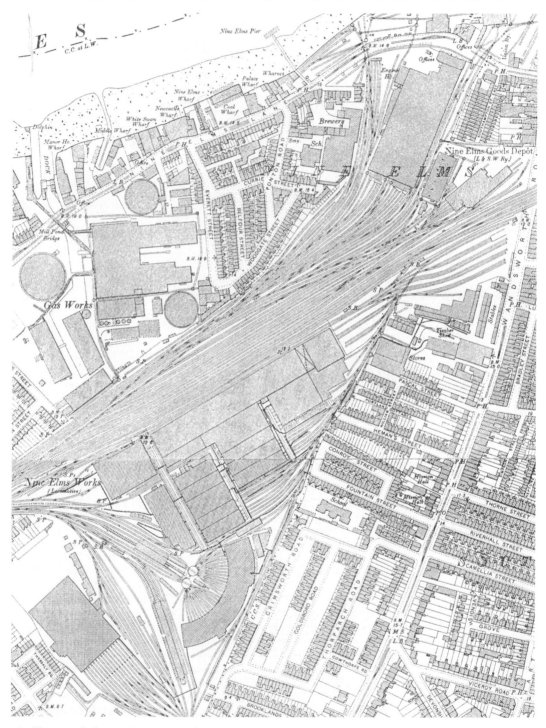

52. The 1894 Ordnance Survey map of Nine Elms shows the amount of land taken up by the railway companies. The goods depot at the top right handled 1.3 million tons of freight in 1913. The locomotive works and depot, south of the main line, could house over 200 engines.

53. The Plough Lane level crossing in 1874.

1860. Although adjacent to the LSWR for almost one mile, no immediate steps were taken to provide a station, nor were the lines physically connected.

The 1860s saw furious railway-building activity in south London, and the local network was completed by 1867, along with additional locomotive sheds, goods facilities and workshops. Scores of acres virtually untouched by development were acquired by the various companies – empty, flat land was the principal reason for the choice of Battersea for these facilities, the nearest to the termini at Waterloo and Victoria. Battersea's third mainline railway arrived in August 1862, when the London, Chatham & Dover Railway (LCDR) opened its line from Beckenham Junction to Victoria.

BUILDING CLAPHAM JUNCTION

Six months later, on 2 March 1863, one of Battersea's most famous landmarks – Clapham Junction - opened for business when the LSWR and the London, Brighton & South Coast Railway (LBSCR, which had absorbed the WECPR) finally acknowledged the need for a traffic interchange where the lines to Richmond, Southampton and Brighton diverged.

Typically, the station was named after the ostensibly more fashionable suburb of Clapham, causing Bradshaw to insert a footnote in its timetable warning unsuspecting travellers that the station lay in mid-Battersea, 1½ miles away. A brief campaign to get the station renamed Battersea Junction failed to overturn what had already become an established fact. Clapham Junction station had been partly built in 1860, and was always an interchange station, rather than a true junction. A restricted physical connection between the two companies was never used for regular services and there were separate LSWR and LBSCR buildings and staffs until 1923. The companies enlarged and rebuilt their stations

54. *The complex of railway tracks leading into Clapham Junction railwy station is amply demonstrated here in 1907. To the right new track is being laid on the Windsor line.*

55. *The high level entrance to Clapham Junction station, St John's Hill, completed in 1910 for the LBSCR.*

56. A bemused passenger in the subway passage at Clapham Junction station. It led to the 17 platforms operated then by several companies who had not numbered the platforms consecutively. From Punch 21 July 1883.

several times, reaching their final form in 1910. From the start, the widely scattered platforms were connected by a footbridge at the west end, and a subway at the east. The latter was narrow, badly lit and the source of endless confusion and complaints, although it was over forty years before the railways were prepared to enlarge it.

The West London Extension Railway (WLER), opened on 2 March 1863, was the first link between the northern and southern systems in London. Initially opened as the West London Railway in 1844 it connected only a junction at Willesden with the basin of the Kensington Canal at Addison Road. It ran, as contemporaries noted, from nowhere to nowhere, and its fortunes only improved when a bridge was built in 1863 to carry the line over to Clapham Junction. By then, it was owned by a number of companies – the Great Western and London & North Western (one-third each), and the LSWR and LBSCR (one-sixth each). The WLER ended with four spurs, one to each side of Clapham Junction, to Waterloo and to Victoria (LCDR).

The local network was completed in 1866-67, when the LBSCR and LCDR opened high-level viaducts across the LSWR, thereby obviating the steep gradients on the original lines from low-lying north Battersea up to Grosvenor Bridge. The Brighton company's South London Line, from Battersea Park to Peckham Rye was part of the same package, providing a cross-suburban route from Victoria to London Bridge linking burgeoning centres like Brixton, Battersea and Peckham.

Battersea's nodal position on the south London rail network, as well as the rapidly-growing local population, which had reached 50,000 by the time the last line was opened, meant that it was well provided, as will be seen below, with passenger and goods stations, although only three of the former and none of the latter remain open today.

Station	Company	Open
Nine Elms	LSR	1838-1848
Wandsworth/		
Clapham Common	LSR	1838-1863
Wandsworth Common	WECPR	1856-1858
New Wandsworth	LBSCR	1858-1869
Pimlico & Battersea	LBSCR	1858-1860
Stewarts Lane	LBSCR	1858
Battersea Park &		
Steamboat Pier	LBSCR	1860-1870
Battersea	WLER	1863-1940
Clapham Junction	LSWR/	
	LBSCR	1863-date
Stewarts Lane	LCDR	1863-1866
York Road/		
Battersea Park	LBSCR	1867-date
Battersea Park Road	LCDR	1867-1916
Queen's Road	LSWR	1877-date

Goods were handled at Nine Elms (LSWR), Battersea Wharf (LBSCR), New Wandsworth (LBSCR), Stewarts Lane (LCDR), Falcon Lane (North-Western), Wandsworth Road (Midland) and South Lambeth (GWR). Building materials and coal were the two major Victorian freight traffics.

Space precludes a detailed analysis of train services, which had a relatively limited impact on housing development in Battersea until the 1880s. Unfortunately, there are no coherent data on fares and loadings to relate to the timetable.

Bradshaw's timetables enable one to chart the growth of services. In September 1875, 451 trains called at Clapham Junction on weekdays, in August 1887, 518, and in April 1899, 565, a growth rate of about 10% per decade. The increase during the Edwardian era, to 665 trains in April 1910 (+18%) was much more rapid, reflecting the maturity of the railway network and the growth in suburban commuting. The use of larger carriages, slowly changing from four- and six-wheel wooden-bodied oil-lit types to bogie coaches with gas lighting, together with longer trains, probably represented a doubling in capacity between 1875 and 1910.

Then as now, the great termini of Waterloo and Victoria were the key destinations, with 45-50% of all trains going there. A dozen trains a day provided a link to Ludgate Hill in the City, albeit by a roundabout route taking in much of inner south London. Kensington was served by forty or so trains provided from the two extremes of the Junction, which no doubt accounts for some of the stories of lost passengers wandering the subway! About one train in eight served the Richmond-Windsor-Reading axis, from what was essentially a separate station on the north side. The greatest growth from 1875-1910 was in services to the south-west (especially the suburbs from Wimbledon outwards), and down the Brighton main line. The original WECPR route from Balham to Norwood remained virtually constant at 55-60 trains per day.

The South London Line (LBSCR) was electrified on the overhead system in 1909 in a successful bid to counter tramway and motor bus competition; this was extended to Croydon and Sutton in 1911. The LSWR followed suit with its inner suburban services in 1915-16, using a d.c. third-rail system, to which the LBSCR lines were converted in the 1920s, leaving behind traces of the overhead wire supports as evidence for the observant traveller.

57. Wandsworth Common station shortly after the 1911 electrification of the LBSCR line into Victoria station. The overhead catenary collection system was replaced by the third rail in 1929.

The LSWR, LCDR and LBSCR all had large engine sheds in Battersea. The LSWR built locomotives at Nine Elms from 1843 to 1909, and the LCDR at Longhedge Works from 1869 to 1911. From all this, railway employment became very important indeed in the local economy. From only 65 individuals in 1851, expansion was rapid: 367 in 1861, 1,142 in 1871, 2,311 in 1881 and 3,130 in 1891. Operations and track maintenance accounted for 55-60% after 1861, works and engine sheds for 20-30%, unspecified clerks and labourers for 8-11%. In 1861, 158 men were engaged in constructing the WLER: 138 navvies, 7 excavators and 3 carmen, a forgeman, horsekeeper, enginewright and two clerks of works. Most came from rural southern England (54% from the Home Counties and south-west, 18% from East Anglia), attracted no doubt by the high wages; only one was born in Ireland.

Despite the growth in absolute numbers after 1871, it was during the formative years, between 1840 and 1867, that the growth rate of railway employment outstripped that of the total population. There was a heavy concentration of railway workers in Nine Elms and adjacent areas, although this proportion declined sharply from 92% in 1851 to 79% in 1861 and to 55-60% after 1871, as Clapham Junction became so important. There was no railway company housing built in Battersea, though much of the local housing was aimed at this sort of skilled working-class market. Some compulsorily purchased houses were held by railway companies, notably eight houses in Brighton Terrace, whose fronts were less than six feet from the South London Line viaduct. Railwaymen relied on the speculative housing market for accommodation. An example of local concentration is provided by Sussex (later Wadhurst) Street, begun in 1850 and with an entrance to Nine Elms works at the end.

Higher than average and regular wages placed railwaymen in a secure position. Charles Booth indicates that there were about 2,600 railway workers in Battersea c.1890, although he understates the position by excluding some unskilled workers. The Board of Trade survey of 1887 had 9.5% employed on the railways, but was biased towards the upper end of the working-class hierarchy, and does not identify precisely those in railway engineering. With weekly earnings of 30s 5d, engine drivers paid 7s in rent and occupied three rooms; 97% were in regular employment, a figure matched only by other railwaymen and the police.

ON THE ROADS

Before the coming of the railway, Battersea enjoyed a very limited coach and cart service to London. In 1823, three coaches a day left the Raven Inn in Battersea Square and three more departed from the Castle in the High Street, a total of about seventy seats at a cost which excluded virtually all of the local populace. In addition, there were daily carriers' carts to a variety of City taverns. Battersea Rise was served by coaches and carts passing by en route to villages further out. Things were getting better, however, and by 1829, the year in which the omnibus made its appearance in London, H. Philpott was providing eight return trips from Battersea with a fifteen-seater coach (compare nineteen trips to Wandsworth).

ON THE BUSES

Like local railways, the bus network developed only slowly. In May 1851, Battersea was served by the following horse bus services: (1) Wandsworth Road-Battersea New Town-Gracechurch Street, half-hourly, 30 minute journey, fare 6d; (2) Wandsworth-St John's Hill-Lavender Hill-Gracechurch Street, 22 buses a day, fare 1/-; (3) Wandsworth Road-Oxford Street, 4 buses a day, fare 6d; (4) Wandsworth-Battersea Bridge-Bank, 3 buses a day, fare 9d. (Wandsworth-Battersea 4d; Battersea-Charing Cross 4d.).

Times, frequencies and fares put these services out of the reach of the vast majority of local people. Despite the formation of the London General Omnibus Co. in 1856 and the rapid expansion of the system, Battersea remained poorly served by buses. In December 1870, John Martin ran one bus between Battersea Bridge and Gracechurch Street via Vauxhall, with four round trips on weekdays and five on Saturdays and the first bus did not leave Battersea until 9am. In April 1876, when Battersea's population was about 90,000, the Suburban Omnibus Co. began a service between Wandsworth and Vauxhall via York Rd. and Battersea Park Road. It ran hourly, but would have been little used by the people living in the densely-packed streets along its route. This company also ran a 2d. feeder from the Northcote in Battersea Rise, an area of lower-middle class estates, to the William IV pub in Wandsworth Road, starting point of the traditional services. In the 1880s, Thomas Tilling of Peckham took over the Clapham-Balham-Tooting service, and reduced the fares.

By 1895 bus services in Battersea had improved in quantity and price, although their timings and relatively high cost ensured that they still catered for an essentially middle-class market. The following then operated: Northcote-Battersea Bridge-Knightsbridge (General), 10-12 mins., journey 39 mins., 26 seats, 4.6mph; Bedford Road-Clapham-Rise-Wandsworth-Putney (Tilling); 20 mins., journey 50 mins., 28 seats, 5.4mph. (Clapham-Falcon 2d, Leathwaite Road-Clapham Junction 1d); Clapham Junction.-Balham Station. (Tilling); 15 mins., journey 15 mins., 12 seats, 7mph.

The total number of seats per day in each direction was 3,500, which is tiny for a population of 160,000.

Local transport in 1895 was dominated by trams and trains, and the concentration of buses in central and south Battersea reflects their higher status and the failure of trams to penetrate south of Lavender Hill.

TRAMS

The tramway age in south London began in earnest in 1870, and by 1890 a network radiating from the Thames bridges had been created by several companies. The South London Tramways Co. (SLT) obtained an Act in 1879, with powers to construct lines from Vauxhall to Lavender Hill and from Plough Lane to Nine Elms. The Wandsworth Board obtained clauses to require the company to pave the whole roadway at passing places, and convey excavated material free to its yard. The 1880 SLT Act authorised lines from the Falcon to the Prince's Head, and from Plough Lane to Wandsworth.

Services began on 1 January 1881, between the Prince's Head and the Royal Rifleman, extended from 12 March to give a Falcon-Nine Elms service, 2.75 miles of mainly single track with passing places. The first trams were 28 forty-seat double-deck cars, about 50% larger than contemporary buses. They were pulled by a stud of 108 horses, and housed in a depot in Queens Road. As the

58. Laying and cementing the LCC electric tram tracks near Christchurch, Battersea Park Road, in 1905.

59. Horse-drawn tram of the South London Tramway Co. on the Clapham Junction to Chelsea Bridge route, at the Chelsea Bridge terminus c.1895.

network grew, additional depots were provided at Clapham Junction station, Gonsalva Road, and Jews Row, Wandsworth.

The following services were offered in 1882: Falcon-Nine Elms every 10 mins., journey 20 mins; Prince's Head-Chelsea Steamboat Pier every 10 mins. A five-minute frequency was provided along Battersea Park Road (*c*.6,700 seats in total per day each way), far better than the parallel railway, although the starting times were akin to those of the buses. Workmen's tickets were available, and ordinary fares were 1d-2d, about 1d a mile.

The 'Upper Road' opened in June 1882, from East Hill, Wandsworth to Westbury Street, Clapham, and extended to Vauxhall in 1883. The York Road-Wandsworth section also opened in 1883, along with extensions to Westminster Bridge and the Hop Exchange in the Borough, which gave access to the City. Piecemeal opening led to poor financial results. Passing places were criticised as being poorly sited and insufficient, and nine more were added in 1886-7. By the 1890s, the whole of Falcon Lane was double track.

In 1895 the horse tram network was at its peak, soon to be taken over by the London County Council and electrified. Routes were identified by colour: Wandsworth-York Road-Battersea Park Road-Westminster Bridge (blue); Wandsworth-York Road-Battersea Park Road-Hop Exchange (green); East Hill-Lavender Hill-Westminster Bridge (yellow); East Hill-Lavender Hill-Hop Exchange (brown); Chelsea Bridge-Clapham Junction (chocolate); Chelsea Bridge-Queens Road-Lavender Hill (red). Trams, seating 40-46 passengers, ran every five-ten minutes and fares averaged ½d to 1d a mile. The hours of operation were usually 7.30am to 10.30pm. Workmen's trams at reduced fares were provided early in the morning on several routes as early as from 5.15am and these ran only along the 'Lower Road' (Battersea Park Road), reflecting the higher social status of Lavender Hill. The total number of seats provided was 480 a day, far less than on local workmen's trains, indicating that here at least the tram did not provide a mass-transit system for artisans. Trams did, however, provide a very good off-peak service, with one every couple of minutes between the Princes Head and Queens Road and every 2½ minute's along St John's Hill-Lavender Hill. Most local trips cost 1d-2d. The SLT also ran buses from Chelsea Bridge to Sloane Square in Chelsea, the nearest point on the Underground.

The LCC bought out the SLT in 1902. Conversion to electric traction began in 1903, using the

60. *An LCC electric tram on Lavender Hill c.1912.*

61. *A no. 12 LCC tram negotiating the Mill Creek bridge in Nine Elms Lane, September 1950. The overhead coal conveyors supplied fuel to the Nine Elms gasworks on the left.*

62. The Prince's Head c.1904, one of the Battersea starting points for trams.

expensive conduit system forced on the LCC by the hostility of local councils to overhead wiring. The local network was converted between 1906 and 1911, and slightly extended along Battersea Bridge Road and across to Chelsea. Other improvements included the reduction of tram workers' hours to sixty a week and the raising of their wages from 4d to 6d per hour. New ½d fare stages were introduced, reducing the cost of certain journeys, for example Wandsworth-Westminster from 3d to 2½d.

STEAMBOATS

By 1851 regular services between Battersea and the City were provided by the London, Westminster & Vauxhall Iron Steamboat Co. (founded 1837) and the City Steam Packet Co. (founded in 1845 and referred to as the Citizen Steamboat Co.). A ten-minute service was offered for 3d, far more frequent than buses and trains and about one-third the price. Battersea had piers at Nine Elms (the embarkation point for rail passengers 1838-48), the Red House, the British Flag and the Old Swan next to Battersea church. Citizen had a boatyard close to Battersea Bridge by 1850, where its fleet of vessels was maintained and in some cases built: for example, the replacements for *Citizen A-F* and *J* during the 1860s. In 1862 the London Steamboat Co. was registered with a capital of £100,000 to take over the Iron and City Steamboat Companies.

After 1880 increased railway and new tram competition seems to have told on the regular river traffic, as did the freeing of the local bridges from tolls in 1878-80. The London Steamboat Co. went into liquidation in 1884 and in 1887 regular services between Battersea and Woolwich ceased and thirty vessels were laid-up. By 1890 services were virtually restricted to the summer pleasure business.

At the end of the nineteenth century, a committee of the London County Council recom-

63. River steamers at Nine Elms pier c.1845. The railway terminus at Nine Elms is hidden behind the warehouse and windmill.

64. *The fleet of the City Steam Boat Co. passing in review order off Chelsea, viewed from Battersea Bridge c.1859.*

mended the provision of a municipal service and the freeing of the piers from tolls. An Act was obtained in August 1904, just when the extension of trams along the Embankment was imminent and the electrification of tramways was adding further to the competition for steamboats. Thirty new vessels were built for the LCC, and operations began in June 1905. Battersea to London was 2d-3d single and 3d-5d return, undercutting rail, bus and tram. A workmen's boat ran from Hammersmith at 5am, calling at all piers; the regular fifteen-minute service ran from 7am until 7.15pm. Some express boats called only at Westminster, Nine Elms and Battersea between London Bridge and Putney.

However, there was a loss of £30,000 in 1905 and the service became a political issue on the Council between the Progressives and the Municipal Reformers. It was suspended in the winter of 1906-7, and ceased after September 1907. Despite carrying 5.5 million passengers in 1906-7, the service lost nearly £74,000 in three years. No subsequent attempt to provide a regular service from outside central central London has succeeded.

Battersea's Churches

Possibly the earliest reference to a church at Battersea is in 1067 AD when King William granted to Westminster Abbey the Manor of 'Batriceseia' where three villages are listed with their churches but does not necessarily imply that each had a church. The earliest firm date for a separate church in Battersea is in a Papal Bull of AD1157, in which "the church of Patriches and the chapel of Wandleswrth" are mentioned.

The date of the first Battersea parish church of St Mary is unknown, but we do know that the foremost medieval architect, Henry Yevele, who constructed the nave of Westminster Abbey, also rebuilt the east gable of St Mary's - the shape of his east window is still apparent in the present church.

Details of village life have survived from the churchwardens' accounts, almost complete from 1559. These include figures for plague deaths in 1578 and 1593. We are told that the archery butts were repaired in 1573 and that in 1580 the church was robbed and the "locke of the church-door" had to be mended. In 1567 we have an expenditure "ffor dryvyng Ye dogs owt of Ye church", a task that recurred many times. A new tower was erected in 1639 at a cost of £469 16s 8d, the bricks being supplied by "Robert Taylor of Latchmeare in Battersea". In 1666 a collection at Battersea raised £12 8s 9d towards "Ye relief of Ye citty of London upon Ye account of Ye fire".

The spoiling of the monasteries instigated by Henry VIII, in the name of reform but in fact to lay claim to their wealth, was continued by Edward VI. In 1548 he ordered a survey of all valuable items of plate, ornaments and vestments held in churches. The Battersea churchwardens, Rowland Jackson and Richard Browne were to forestall the commissioners by selling in 1549 a chalice and other articles for £7 17s 2d which they spent on a new pulpit and repairs to the church. The church was still well endowed and in 1552 the commissioners were to seize altar cloths, vestments and articles of copper and pewter. The parson's messuage (house and land) is mentioned in 1636 as "belonging to the Rectorie a faire house with a Barne orchard and garden" as well as "a viccaridge house with an orchard and garden two barnes and two outehouses".

The marriage register records that William and Edmund Burke witnessed the wedding of John Ridge and Catherine Somner Sedley on 4 October 1757. William Blake, the poet, artist and mystic married Catherine Butcher (or Boucher) on 18 August 1782. His wife was the daughter of a Battersea market gardener. "She proved herself one of the best wives that ever befell to the lot of a man of genius", according to the *Dictionary of National Biography*.

On 15 May 1800 were married James Stephen of the Middle Temple and Sarah Clarke by John Venn of Clapham in the presence of William Wilberforce and his wife Barbara Ann Wilberforce. The bride was Wilberforce's sister and the bridegroom was his brother-in-law. All of those at the ceremony were prominent members of the 'Clapham Sect' *(see p138)* and slave trade abolitionists.

St Mary's was totally rebuilt in 1777 to the designs of the architect Joseph Dixon and the building work was done by his brother Richard Dixon. The new building incorporated the 17th-century window depicting the family pedigree of Oliver St John and Viscount Grandison who bought title to the Manor in 1627. Monuments

65. St Mary's Church as rebuilt, with the Swan Inn to the left. Drawing by J. Cullum.

66. *Monument to Sir Edward Wynter (d.1685), placed on the south wall of the rebuilt church.*

67. *Christchurch, as depicted in the Illustrated London News, 10 February, 1849.*

include those to Sir Oliver St John, Viscount Grandison (died 1630) and to Henry St John, Viscount Bolingbroke (died 1751).

The most astonishing memorial is that to Sir Edward Wynter, Battersea's own Baron Munchausen, who died on 2 March 1685 at York House. The white marble relief depicts Sir Edward strangling a tiger. Part of the caption reads:

> Not less in martiall honour was his name: Witness his actions of immortal fame: Alone, anarm'd a Tygre He oppresst; And crush'd to death Ye Monster of a Beast; Thrice-twenty mounted Moors he overthrew. Singly on foot, some wounded, some he slew, Dispersd Ye rest: what more cou'd Sampson do? True to his friends, a Terrour to his Foes, Here, now, in peace his honour'd bones repose.

The artist J.M.W. Turner painted many of his cloud scenes from the vestry oriel window and his chair is on display there today. Benedict Arnold, one of George Washington's generals in the American War of Independence, defected to the British side and was buried here in 1801. A stained glass window has been erected in his memory.

NEW CHURCHES

As the population expanded and the parish church became inadequate, extra space was created by the opening of St George's-in-the-Fields at Nine Elms, designed by Edward Blore. Nearer the village in 1849 was built Christchurch, with its tall spire, in Battersea Park Road. An attempt to provide for the factory workers of the York Road district was made with the erection of St John's in Usk Road in 1863 – services were previously held in a room at Price's Candle Factory. St Paul's on St John's Hill, costing £6,300, was consecrated in 1868.

Philip W. Flower donated the site for St Philip's in Queenstown Road at the centre of his Park Town estate. Costing £13,000, the church, designed by James Knowles, opened in 1870. The parish of Christchurch was divided by the opening of St Saviour's, Battersea Park Road in 1871.

The energetic new vicar of Battersea in 1872, John Erskine Clarke, formerly at St Andrew's Derby, was to oversee the construction and open-

68. St Philip's church, Queenstown Road c.1910. The single-deck trams were in service until 1927, when the railway bridges near Queens Road station were rebuilt to allow double-deck trams through.

ing of eleven more churches. He was an enthusiastic bell ringer and within six months had the Waterloo Society of Change-ringers perform a peal of Grandsire Triples of 5,040 changes, and six months later had founded the St Mary's Amateur Ringers. He was also the originator of the first parish magazine, produced by him in the 1860s.

The first of his new buildings, in 1874, was St Mark's on Battersea Rise. Designed by William White, it replaced a small iron church that was then transferred to Nightingale Lane to become the nucleus of St Luke's church.

In fairly quick succession were built the following: St Peter's, Plough Road (1876); St Matthew's, Gowrie Road (1876); Ascension Church, Lavender Hill (started 1876 and completed 1893); St Michael's, Bolingbroke Grove (1881); St Mary-le-Park, Albert Bridge Road (1883, which was intended as a new parish church but was never completed); All Saints', Queenstown Road (1884); St Stephen's, Battersea Bridge Road (1885); St Andrew's, Patmore Street (1886); St Luke's, Thurleigh Road (1889); St Barnabas, North Side, Clapham Common (1898).

Canon Clarke retired in 1909 and a plaque in St Mary's was erected to mark his work in the parish.

69. St Mark's church, Battersea Rise c.1910. The smaller building on the right is St Mark's Infants' school, built 1866 for the parish of St Mary but allotted to St Mark's when the church was built 1872-74.

NONCONFORMISTS

Thomas Horrocks organised a meeting of Baptists in Battersea in 1672. A Baptist Meeting House was erected in York Road in 1736 and their first church was built in 1797 and rebuilt in 1870. Israel May Soule, minister of the Baptist Chapel from 1838 to 1875, was dubbed the 'Bishop of Battersea' and it was said of him that "he was a Baptist minister, but of such a catholic spirit that he worked most cordially with members of other churches and regardless of sectarian distinction and differences, was ever ready to co-operate with churchmen in all good works." A large obelisk was erected above his grave in Battersea cemetery, Bolingbroke Grove. A 'New' Baptist church was built in Chatham Road in the 1860s and others in Battersea Park Road and Meyrick Road. The Northcote Road Baptist chapel was opened in 1889.

Prior to 1845 the Methodists met in private houses and worshipped in an upper room above a joiner's shop in King Street, now part of Westbridge Road near the Raven. They completed their first church in that road about 1845, enlarging it in 1864 and again in 1871. The Queenstown Road church was built in 1881 and others soon appeared, in Battersea Church Road, Mallinson Road, Grayshott Road and Broomwood Road.

The Congregational Church in Battersea Bridge Road was opened in 1867 and two others were built in Cabul and Stormont Roads.

The Catholic community purchased no. 5 (now 36) Altenburg Gardens for their chapel but chose the neighbouring orchard as the site for a church: St Vincent de Paul was opened in 1907. Elsewhere the Countess of Stockport donated £700 for construction of an iron church in Trott Street in 1875. The present Church of the Sacred Heart was designed by F.A. Walters and opened in 1893. The Church of Our Lady of Mount Carmel in Battersea Park Road was built in 1868. Associated with the church was the convent of Notre Dame and a boys' and girls' school.

The Salesian Catholic College acquired Surrey

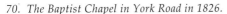

70. The Baptist Chapel in York Road in 1826.

71. *Battersea Park Tabernacle, Battersea Park Road, c.1904.*

Lodge in Surrey Lane in 1895 and has since expanded considerably, taking in boys from 11 to 16.

The Salvation Army had a citadel in the High Street and also took over the former Park Town Hall in Prairie Street.

Battersea must have seemed a godless pit with the need for the many mission churches and chapels that appeared throughout the district at the end of the 19th century. In the 1902/3 Mudie-Smith census of religious undertakings there are 18 Anglican churches and 51 other chapels, churches and mission rooms. The maximum attendance at evening services was 14,605, which represents only 8-9% of the 1901 population, a far lower figure than expected at the end of the Victorian era.

In recent times attendance has reduced and many of the mission halls and churches have closed. The South West London Synagogue, opened in a house on Bolingbroke Grove about 1920, was closed in 2000. St Bartholomew's church, Wycliffe Road, opened in 1902 was taken over by the Greek Orthodox Church in 1971 and given the name St Nectarios.

72. *The Wesleyan Methodist church, Broomwood Road c.1910. It was demolished c.1986 and replaced by Ash Court c.1987, a Methodist Homes Housing scheme.*

73. *Speke Hall, Speke Road, headquarters of the Pentecostal League founded by Reader Harris KC in 1891, to spread scriptural holiness by non-sectarian methods. Mary Harris wrote* Spiritual Realities, *published 1922 in Battersea.*

74. *The gospel van of the Church of Christ, Battersea c.1908. "For the spread of the Gospel according to the Scriptures" is painted on the van panelling.*

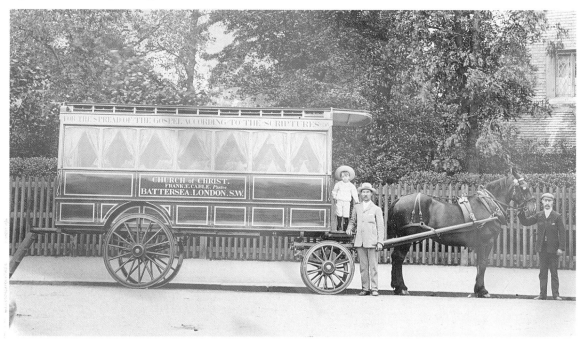

Open Spaces

CLAPHAM COMMON

The Commons were owned by the Lord of the Manor but his tenants (copyholders) had rights to graze animals on them, to let their pigs loose to forage, or to gather wood for specific purposes. The boundary between Battersea and Clapham, mentioned in a 16th-century sale, was marked by a "bounded ditch made by the inhabittants of Battersay", which ran from Browmell's Corner, from the southern corner of Wix's Lane, to the corner of South Side and Nightingale Lane. Disputes between Battersea and Clapham as to who had control of what is now called Clapham Common arose in 1575 when a Clapham labourer was found on the 'Esteheath' mowing the fern; Battersea residents were soon on the scene and the man and his scythe were sent packing. To emphasise Battersea's superiority in this, a cart was sent along the following day to have the mowed fern removed to the Battersea Manor House.

By the beginning of the 18th century the ditch had become almost obliterated and Clapham farmers allowed their cattle to graze on all parts of the Common, claiming the whole for themselves. Therefore, in 1716 a new ditch was dug by Battersea some six feet beyond the old boundary, which Clapham promptly filled in. The dispute went to court in 1718 and Clapham won but the people of Battersea continued perambulating their old bounds and the boundary between the two parishes still follows approximately the line of the old ditch.

Clapham Common in the 18th century was described as nothing better than a morass with gravel pits and potholes; little grew there except a few trees and gorse bushes. Christopher Baldwin, a West India merchant and magistrate living at Broxash on the west side of the Common was instrumental in levelling, draining and planting it, partly funding this himself with contributions from nearby residents; work was completed by 1760.

Threats to enclose the Common in 1827 and later in the 19th century to put it up for sale as building land were thwarted by local residents and it was purchased in 1877 by the Metropolitan Board of Works and made available to all for recreation. Cast-iron boundary markers erected by Battersea parish, placed at intervals across the Common, from Wix's Lane to the corner of Nightingale Lane can still be discerned.

WANDSWORTH COMMON

What had been Battersea West Heath (now Wandsworth Common) was cut through by the West End of London & Crystal Palace Railway in 1858. The company also purchased more land than it required and sold it for building development such as off Chivalry Road.

In 1857 the Lord of the Manor, Earl Spencer, sold 55 acres to the Royal Victoria Patriotic Asylum. Despite being opposed by campaigners such as John Buckmaster, he was then in the process of enclosing and selling off small parcels of the Common. Buckmaster persuaded James Digby Smith, one of the last copyholders, who occupied a semi-derelict cottage in the Chivalry Road area and who made a living "selling potatoes, brickdust and treacle", to file a lawsuit against Spencer for continued free use of the Common. Petitions to the Earl and to the Metropolitan Board of Works in 1863 and 1868 proved unfruitful, the Board indicating that if they were to take over the Common even more land had to be sold to defray further expenses. In 1869 Buckmaster led a group of about 2000 people to tear down fences erected on the Common near Chivalry Road for building operations. This direct action was called for again on 13 April 1870 when more fences were torn down from Plough Green, now covered by Strathblaine Road.

The formation of a committee in 1870 to oppose Earl Spencer's claim to absolute ownership of the Common was crucial for the future of these remaining open spaces, including Wimbledon Common. The campaign was led by the wealthier inhabitants, but was keenly supported by the working people of Battersea and Wandsworth. The first meeting took place in Battersea where working-class representatives spoke about their hopes for the Common. Local factories raised weekly subscriptions.

Spencer eventually agreed to a meeting with the committee at which he stated that as his income from the Common amounted to £500 per annum, he was entitled to a similar sum in recompense. Mr Ransome feared that the sum was too much to be managed and that as the Common was wanted for public purposes, he thought £250 could be managed by the local community. Subsequently, the sum of £250 was agreed. An Act of Parliament was obtained in July 1871. Independent conservators were appointed "to keep the Common for ever open and unenclosed and unbuilt on ... for purposes of health and unrestricted exercise and recreation".

75. *A view of Battersea Park and its lake in 1858, when it was opened.*

The land was in a poor state with disused gravel pits piled high with rubbish, ponds that stank of foul water, and the paths across the Common were almost non-existent and ditches muddy. The conservators put in hand levelling and planting but locals felt that they were paying twice for the privilege (to the conservators and also to the Board of Works for London commons in general). This resulted in management being transferred in 1887 to the Metropolitan Board of Works. The Commons later came under the control of Wandsworth Borough Council.

BATTERSEA PARK

The idea of establishing a Royal Park in Battersea seems to have come from the great builder-developer, Thomas Cubitt, who saw an opportunity to create a green lung in south-west London before houses and industry covered the area (Victoria Park performed a similar function in north-east London at the same time). Cubitt himself owned some land here, but was not interested in building in this low-lying, often marshy area. He persuaded the government to adopt his scheme, and an Act was obtained in 1846. The project was in the hands of the Commissioners of Woods and Forests, and James Pennethorne, designer of

Victoria Park, was their architect. He had produced his first plans in 1843. These were altered to a more angular design with the available space cut through with a half-mile long avenue on an east-west axis and a simple path from north to south.

The Act scheduled 340 acres for purchase in more than 360 lots, reflecting the fact that most of it consisted of common field strips, although some of the land was never acquired by the Crown. Seven individuals owned 61% of this land. Chief among them were Edward Pain, developer of several estates in Battersea, who had 69 acres, Cubitt (33 acres) and old-establshed local land-owners Thomas Ponton (28), Andrew McKellar (26) and Richard Southby (25). Cubitt had been acquiring land here for some time, but he seems vindicated of the charge of speculating with a view to cashing in on his idea. If anybody did, it was Edward Pain, who more than doubled his holding after 1839. John Cornelius Park, with 15 acres, had begun to build near River Wall (later Parkgate) Road, although his houses were soon demolished.

Only 200 acres were used for the Park. During the slow process of land purchase, levelling and laying out (the Park did not open until 1858), there was a severe downturn nationally in building activity, which affected the subsequent development of the area. A few grand roads were laid out in the vicinity of the Park – Prince of Wales Road (south), Albert Road (west), leading to Albert Bridge after 1873, and Victoria Road (east), leading to Chelsea Bridge.

The railway was extended across the eastern part of the Crown Estate in 1858-60 and this, and the expansion of the Southwark & Vauxhall Waterworks took most of the land east of Victoria Road, nullifying any idea of high-status housing there.

The total cost of the Park by the time it opened was £312,890, of which £246,517 was for land. The Crown paid an average of £800 per acre, far less than owners had hoped for. In December 1847 in a case concerning three acres of Thames bank, the value was reduced from a claim of £10,212 to £750. A jury was called in December 1850 to assess Edward Pain's claim for £94,800 (£1,375 per acre), but he settled out of court for £35,000 (£500 per acre), but still a very handsome return on his outlay of between £4,000 and £6,000.

So protracted were proceedings in purchasing the land that some builders had carried on with developments in the proposed park area. One victim of the delay was Henry Hart Davis, a civil engineer from Chelsea, who set about developing estates with gusto in various parts of Battersea from 1845. Earl Spencer Place lay within the Park area, and Davis claimed £4,875 as early as November 1846, but the dilatoriness of the Crown contributed to his bankruptcy in 1850. A Mr Budge had erected fourteen carcases and claimed compensation, which the judge rejected on the grounds that the Crown was not bound to proceed without funds.

Late in 1851 *The Builder* found the "Battersea wastes still shapeless barrenness". Despite the optimistic forecast of *The Times* that the Park would be ready by the end of 1850, not until the autumn of 1853 were all claims settled and the final demolitions took place. From 1853 auctions were held as properties were demolished and materials were sold. The British Flag and the Red House (for which £11,000 had been allowed) were the last to go before the area was ploughed and manured. Many of the sales within the Park were by W.R. Glasier of Charing Cross, yet another local developer. In February 1853, 660,000 bricks were sold near the Albert Tavern. The Tivoli tea gardens, including a 60ft assembly room and two 80ft barges "with houses on top", followed in August, and the Red House and the neighbour-

ing White Mill and cottage in December. In February 1854 the British Flag and its shooting ground came under the hammer. The sale of the York Depot Drain Pipe and Tile Works in October 1854 yielded tiles, firebricks and stock bricks to potential developers. In November, Glasier sold nine new houses in Carlton Terrace, developed by Edward Pain as recently as 1852. In August 1855 1-2 Grove Villas in Surrey Lane and two "newly-erected gothic houses" in Marsh Lane succumbed. The Hope Tavern lasted until mid-1857, while the materials of the former Albert Tavern within the Park were not sold until 1875.

Queen Victoria opened the Park on 28 March 1858. John Gibson was appointed superintendent in 1856 and worked there for 14 years; 120 men were employed to build a riverside promenade, 120 ft wide the length of the park; three quarters of a million cubic yards of material were brought in to raise the marshy parts to a dry level. The ornamental lake was excavated in 1860 with the associated rock cascade added between 1866 and 1870. Rowing skiffs could be hired and many young couples found solitude here away from prying eyes. The Subtropical Garden was opened in 1864. The growing popularity of the Park, with 40,000 to 50,000 Sunday visitors by 1865, meant the Subtropical Garden and other areas including the lake had to be fenced off. The Park boundary then had only a timber palisade and the cast iron railings were added later. Plantations of 44,058 trees and shrubs plus many thousands of American trees from Kew Gardens accounted for twenty acres of the park. The river embankment was planted with groups of ornamental trees and shrubs.

The Park was the venue in July 1862 for the Royal Agricultural Show. Its heyday was the period from the 1880s to just before the First World War. For those with the means, a favourite pastime was to drive around the Park in a carriage but Battersea was the first London park to allow cycling on its carriage drives and cyclists arrived in increasing numbers and soon outnumbered carriage enthusiasts.

The lake was stocked with carp, roach, bream and perch, an angler's paradise for many years. The lake could be crossed on a wooden rustic bridge, replaced by a stone bridge in the 1920s. Two aviaries held pheasants, owls, finches, pigeons and a raven. The bandstand was so popular that in 1900 extra space was made to seat up to 1,000 for each concert. An enclosure for approximately half a dozen deer was built towards

76. *Ladies gather at the refreshment rooms in Battersea Park in 1895, to join in the new craze of cycling. No "awful garments" – knickerbockers – are on view.*

77. *Two more cyclists in the Park. Another view of 1895.*

78. *A Sunday scene at the boating lake in Battersea Park. From The Sphere, 10 May 1905.*

the eastern edge of the park The exotic plants in the Subtropical Garden included mulberry, Indian rubber and vanilla trees, date and palm, bamboo, banana and pampas. The Japanese Garden had miniature Bonsai trees and other Asian exotics. Each autumn a chrysanthemum show was held in the conservatories. When frozen the lake was used by skaters if the ice was more than 3 inches thick, attendants standing close by with ropes and planks in case of emer-

gency. A firm favourite of Queen Mary, between the two world wars, was the Old English Garden.

The grounds were dug over for allotments during both wars, the grass giving way to vegetable growing. The Royal Aircraft Factory at Farnborough established an experimental department in Battersea Park in late 1914 or early 1915 for research into aerial photography and the use of wireless, gun mountings and ammunition in aircraft. A war memorial, sculpted by Eric Kennington and dedicated to the 24th Division, was unveiled in 1922. The grass was to be sacrificed again in World War Two, not solely for vegetables, but also for rows of army tents, barrage balloons and an anti-aircraft rocket battery based on the eastern side of the Park, not too far from where the wartime pig pens were sited.

The bandstand was to stage many fund-raising and patriotic gatherings such as the Anglo-Soviet week where Mrs Haden Guest gave a rousing speech.

The Royal Engineers constructed a wartime temporary wooden bridge connecting Chelsea with the park; this was erected in case any of the permanent bridges were bombed. Railings and fences were removed for the wartime scrap drive. The brightness returned to the park during its use as the Festival Gardens in 1951. Post-war expenditure on the Park itself was kept to a minimum and it was rather neglected under the control of the LCC and later the Greater London Council. The former funfair site was used for the British Genius Exhibition in 1977, the Queen's Silver Jubilee year. The Peace Pagoda, based on ancient Indian and Japanese Buddhist designs, was unveiled near the riverside in May 1985.

In 1986 the Park came under the control of Wandsworth Borough Council which immediately scheduled improvements. The bandstand and railings, removed during the war, were replaced, the running track was renewed and the tennis courts floodlit to provide all year use. The Council had only just instigated a tree-planting schedule when the Great Storm of October 1987 struck. About 200 trees came crashing down, and fencing and lamp-posts were torn from their

moorings. The Park was a sad sight but the Council repaired the damage swiftly. The 1861 pump and engine house was refurbished and reopened in 1992 as an art gallery, the ground floor of which has a display on the history of the Park.

SOME LOCAL SPACES

Christchurch Gardens, originally laid out by the Metropolitan Gardens Association and opened in 1885, was taken over by the Vestry in 1889, and the Council from 1900. The Gardens were remodelled after bomb damage in the Second World War and a shelter for old people was erected as a war memorial to Battersea people who had lost their lives in the war.

Vicarage Gardens alongside the river Thames, opened in 1896 with a private donation of £1,000, was taken over and managed by the Council

The Latchmere Estate recreation ground in Burns Road, formerly a series of allotments, was opened in 1906; it consists of only 1.5 acres.

79. A tempestuous game of cricket in Battersea Park, as seen by the artist Frank Reynolds for Punch magazine, 6 June 1905. The caption reads: "Garn! The Treasurer goes in before the bloomin' Seckertary!"

An Industrial Place

Although in 1814 the historians Manning & Bray could state that Battersea "land is nearly equally divided between arable (including garden ground) and pasture" it is clear that even then for close on two centuries, the area had experienced the increasing industrialisation affecting all of the south bank of the London Thames, as work moved away from the City. It was often the most odorous and polluting sections of trade that migrated like this. Manufacturing chemists and druggists, for example, had found wharfage and freedom from restrictions to their advantage at Battersea's riverside.

Brickmaking is mentioned in 1639 when Robert Taylor was paid for digging the clay and moulding 195,000 bricks at his kilns at Latchmere for the new church steeple. In 1645 a brewhouse is mentioned at Nine Elms. Three windmills on the riverside are listed, that of Mr Dawes 'whitingmaker' in 1649 for grinding white lead, a corn mill and a 'Coloure' windmill, grinding colours for potters. Two of these mills, one a neighbour of the Red House, the other on the Lambeth boundary, survived into the 19th century.

A wood-yard in 1686 and a 'Lymekill' are listed in 1688; these kilns, which stood near the mill-pond bridge in Nine Elms Lane, were to survive for almost 200 years.

The church owned land in Nine Elms and docks (for timber) were dug in 1733 to provide rent income; by 1774 three docks were providing £70 per annum. Agricultural produce such as melons was taken to London by water transport from the market gardens where fruit and vegetables, especially peas and the first asparagus grown in this country, were cultivated. Medicinal herbs, known as simples were another crop and this led to a now defunct proverb 'You must go to Battersea to get your simples cut', usually addressed to those not very quick witted. A dung wharf west of the Red House took 'night soil' from London as manure for agricultural use. The Nine Elms area was known for its orchards of apple, pear and cherry trees; also grown were gooseberry bushes, currants and roses.

The osier beds on the marshland were used for

80. Windmills and industry at Nine Elms, on the Lambeth boundary, 1829.

basket weaving and mat making; and fishing for salmon was an important form of income. A sugarhouse, where molasses were refined, is mentioned in 1670, John Smith 'Sugar Refyner' is mentioned in 1671 as having been in operation for several years importing sugar from Barbados. Insurance records for 1713 and 1715 list two sugar-houses, one a substantial structure built of brick, six storeys high of 5,384 sq. ft sited between St Mary's and York Place, probably in York Place itself.

A heavily insured undertaking was Edward Webster's turpentine manufactory on the river-side from 1786 to the early 19th century. The insurance premium was noted as hazardous no doubt because the factory was constructed of wood. A copper works was in operation at Nine Elms by 1724. By 1794 there were a least two distilleries; one, belonging to Messrs Hodgson & Co, used the horizontal air mill next to St Mary's for milling their corn. This mill, built in 1790 by Thomas Fowler, was first used for grinding lin-seed oil. It stood a little over 120ft tall and 52ft diameter at the base and used a system of shut-ters to operate a series of vanes inside the struc-ture to drive the six pairs of mill wheels. Adjacent

to the mill was an enclosed ground 600ft by 32ft, for the fattening of oxen, 650 in total.

Mark Bell and Samuel Bishop had warehouses, granaries, still house, millhouse and stables at York Place in 1741; this was possibly the site of the 1713 sugar-house. The still house or distillery was probably to the west of Price's candle fac-tory. As a side enterprise, up to 1,000 pigs were fed from the residue from distillation and a bacon house, butcher's shop, melting house, killing shed, drying stoves and salting house are mentioned in 1762. They also operated the water mill on the Falcon Brook, in the north-east corner of York Place grounds. The distillery continued operat-ing until 1815.

John Fownes established a glove factory in Battersea in 1777. The works, employing up to 600, were originally in Falcon Lane before mov-ing to York Place.

In 1827 Henry Beaufoy purchased fifteen acres in the western fields of Longhedge / Piddoes Farm, now Wickersley and Wycliffe Roads, to found an acetic acid factory – a cheap substitute for brewed vinegar. The factory also produced chlorides of soda and lime. Beaufoy Road appeared in 1879 as part of the gradual encroachment of building

81. The Koh-I-Nor enamel laboratory, Sheepcote Lane, c.1890.

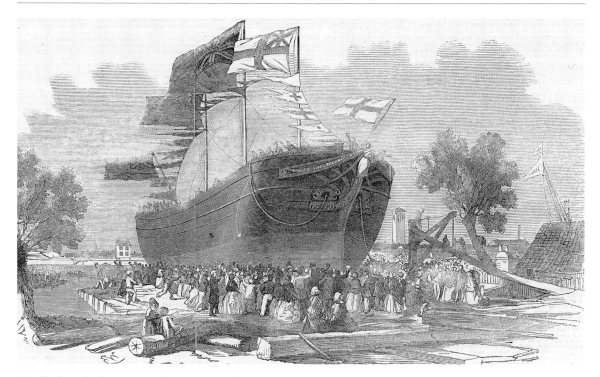

82. *The launch of the Louisa Shelborne from Carne's yard at Nine Elms, April 1854. At 560 tons, the vessel, built for the Baltic trade between London and St Petersburg, was the largest ever constructed upstream of London Bridge.*

development. The factory closed in 1901.

Sir Marc Isambard Brunel (later famous for his Thames tunnel between Wapping and Rotherhithe opened in 1843, and father of Isambard Kingdom Brunel) was introduced to Lord Spencer in 1797, then 1st Lord of the Admiralty. Soon engaged at Portsmouth manufacturing ships' pulley blocks, he built a factory to the west of Battersea Bridge making furniture. He also employed ex-servicemen to manufacture 'seamless boots' for the army at a rate of 100 to 400 pairs per day at 6s 6d per pair. Most of Wellington's troops at Waterloo in 1815 were wearing Brunel's boots. The Brunel works included a saw and veneer mill where two 18ft diameter and two 9ft diameter circular saws were in use. The works burnt down in 1814 and although rebuilt, his partner had squandered much capital and the business failed in 1821. The considerable sum of £60,000 was expended in 1819/20 to erect a soapworks to the east of Battersea Bridge on the waterfront on a site later taken up by Phillip's Waste Paper Mills.

The grounds of York House were used for the famous Battersea Enamel Works from 1750 to the 1770s initiated by Stephen Theodore Jansen. The French artist, Simon Ravenet, was employed here;

he introduced to England the art of transfer printing from copper plates onto enamel. The articles made included snuffboxes, candle sticks, bon-bon boxes, wine labels, buttons and trinkets in the form of birds or animals. Jansen was made bankrupt in 1756; the undertaking proved financially unsound and the contents of the factory were sold off at auction. However, enamels continued in production at Battersea until the 1770s, under the management of John Brooks.

A tide mill at Nine Elms for grinding corn was in use by 1787. Thames water was allowed to fill a large millpond that drove the mill at low tide. Consequently, the mill wheels were in use four times a day. Battersea Park Road had a noticeable hump where the millpond bridge stood, only removed in the 1980s.

William Pamplin set up his nursery business in 1820 on both sides of what is now Lavender Hill to cultivate herbs and lavender for the perfume industry. In the 1820s the road was just the Road to London but was soon known as Lavender Hill.

Allied to the introduction of the railway at Nine Elms in 1838 was the building of two steamboat piers to take passengers onwards to London. Wharves and warehouses were soon added to cater for the Portland stone delivered for the many building works in London. Nine Elms was rapidly filling with industry by the 1850s. The Iron Boat works of the 1850s were launching merchant ships on the Thames destined for use in the Baltic, and in May 1862, the Citizen Steam Boat Co launched its sixteenth vessel from its Battersea boatyard. Other barge builders were busy at Nine Elms and near the parish church.

The London Gas Light Co. of Vauxhall built a gas producing plant in Nine Elms Lane and began manufacturing gas there in 1858. The works covered 17 acres and backed onto the LSWR railway lines which carried away the coke. On 31 October 1865 ten men were killed when a gasholder exploded. The holder, of 1,039,000 cu.ft., 150ft diam and 60ft high, also damaged nearby holders and demolished properties in neighbouring streets. The company had extensive docking facilities to unload coal from barges and about 15,000 tons were stock piled at the works. The

by-products, tar, naphtha, ammonia, benzol etc had their own distribution networks. They also built The Field gasholder station in Prince of Wales Road in 1872; the tall waterless gasholder was added in the 1930s.

The Southwark and Vauxhall Water Co. occupied almost 50 acres to the east of the later Grosvenor Railway Bridge. Its works comprised six water-filtering beds and two reservoirs of about ten acres containing 46 million gallons. In 1850 the water was drawn from the Thames at Battersea but in 1855, after health legislation following cholera outbreaks, was taken at Hampton and pumped to the works. The works were relocated in the 1920s and the site was chosen for the Battersea Power Station, but the 1850s pumping station in Kirtling Street survives. It is interesting to note that the village pump in Battersea Square was not finally closed until March 1877 after analysis condemned the supply.

Orlando Jones & Co, starch works was built

83. *The ruins and debris after the explosion at Nine Elms gasworks on 31 October 1865. The gasholder held over 1,000,000 cubic feet of gas and was almost full when the explosion occurred.*

84. *The scrubbers, part of the gas purifying process, Nine Elms gas works c.1879.*

85. *The works of the Southwark & Vauxhall Water Company at Battersea, depicted in 1884.*

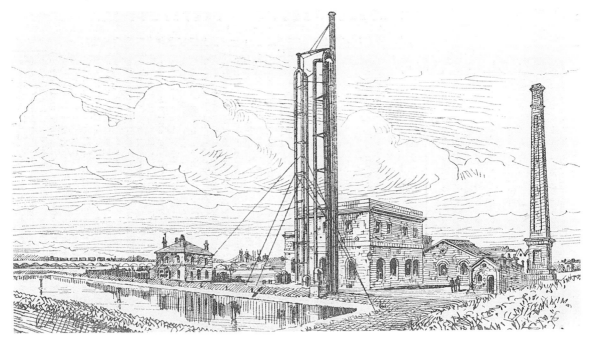

86. Cleaning a filter bed at the Southwark & Vauxhall Water Company's works at Battersea, c.1902.

87. The Orlando Jones Starch Factory c.1850s. Coal is being unloaded from one barge directly onto the wharf while two more barges are loaded with the finished products.

near to Price's candles on the waterfront in 1848. Orlando Jones discovered a method of extracting starch from rice by the use of caustic potash or soda. The rice was brought upriver and discharged at the company's wharf from where the finished article was exported. A great demand for their product emanated from the large-scale local laundries in the 1870s. The works closed in 1901.

H. Young & Co., engineers, founders and smiths, based at Foundry Wharf, Nine Elms had cast many fine statues such as that of Lord Derby, placed opposite the House of Lords and the Wellington Memorial in St Paul's cathedral. When a London pharmacist, Thomas Whiffen, joined the fine chemicals makers, Herring & Hulle in 1834 this was the beginning of the well-known Battersea chemical firm, Whiffen & Son Ltd, operating from Lombard Road. A pharmacist named Price was active, from 1749, in the manufacture of fine chemicals and pharmaceuticals. His business was continued by John May in 1834, who was joined shortly by William Garrard Baker to found the famous firm of May & Baker Ltd at Garden Wharf, next to Price's candles.

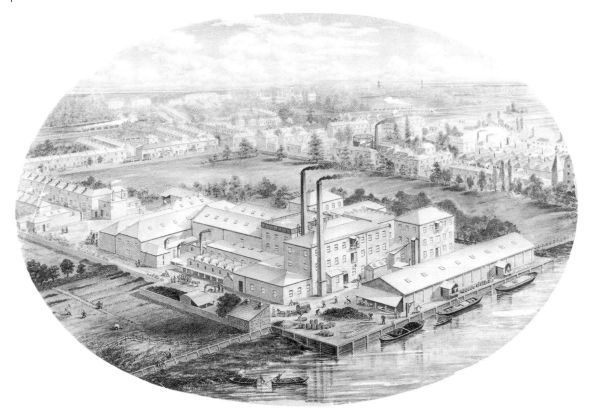

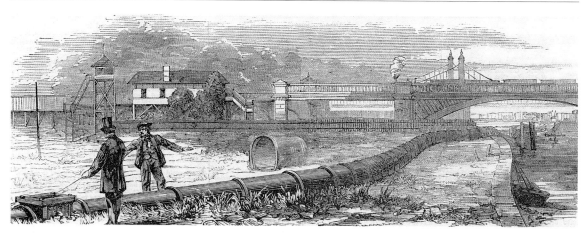

88. *Experimental trials by the Pneumatic Dispatch Co. of a pneumatic letter and parcel railway which took place by the Thames near the Southwark & Vauxhall Co.'s filter beds, in August 1861. The underground railway using this technology was later built between Euston Station and Eversholt Street sorting office in Camden Town.*

89. *Advertisement for the Pure Water Company of Queenstown Road c.1900.*

PRICE'S CANDLES

Battersea's famous candle firm, Price and Co. began trading as Edward Price & Co. in 1830 in a small factory in Vauxhall. Larger premises were sought and the site of York House by the riverside, the old mansion of the Archbishop of York and more latterly of the enamel works, was taken up in 1843. The firm saw the import of palm oil from West Africa as helping to undermine the slave trade, a director writing that "it pays the King better to employ their people in palm-oil collecting than to sell them as slaves". Reformed as Price's Patent Candle Co in 1847, the factory, known as Belmont Works, was by the 1870s to cover 13½ acres fronting York Road and the Thames. In 1882, 1,000 people were employed and this had increased to 1,400 by 1896. Awarded many medals at international exhibitions, the firm's output was phenomenal: in 1877 they produced 147 million candles, 32 million night lights, almost one million gallons of lamp oil and also a large range of household and toilet soaps. The widespread introduction of gas and electric lighting led to a decline in use of the company's candle products so the company branched out into manufacturing motor oils, soap and white spirit. Their products enjoyed a small surge in sales during the early 1970s, as strikes hit the consumption of electricity but, increasingly, candle production was based overseas and the Belmont Works was relegated to showroom and distribution status. The site was largely sold off for housing development in the late 1990s and only a small retail outlet and showroom remain of the once mighty works.

90. *The candle-room at Price's Candle Factory in November 1861.*

MORGAN CRUCIBLE

The Patent Plumbago Crucible Co. was founded in 1856, by the six older Morgan brothers (there were nine in total). Octavius was to be Battersea's first MP and Walter, later Sir Walter, was to be Lord Mayor of London. The company set up a crucible and refractory materials factory in a former pottery on the riverside in Church Road. By 1862 the firm had constructed a purpose built factory with a 100ft tall Italianate clock tower and also a river wall to enable graphite and clay to be unloaded at their own wharf. The staff had increased to 150 by 1872 and the firm's name was changed to Morgan Crucible Co, though it was known locally until closure in the 1970s as 'The Plum'. The firm introduced a pension scheme in 1883 and holiday pay in 1891. The products were crucial during the 1897 Klondike Gold Rush and by 1900 the staff had increased to 421 and the company had Battersea 2 as its telephone number. Diversifying into electrical brushes in 1903 and

carbon arcs for lamps in the 1930s, the company employed nearly 5,000 during World War Two production of searchlight and radio components.

In 1874 the Vestry had to call on the Wandsworth District of Works to abate or remove the nuisance caused by an ammonia works in Lombard Road. The Board sought legal opinion in respect of the alum and ammonia works and Whiffen's factory. The advice was to hire an eminent chemist to make an inspection.

The colour of workers faces would denote their trade - black from Morgan's Crucible, yellow from the Projectile (*see below*) and white from the flourmills.

WORK FOR WOMEN

Employment opportunities for women increased with the advent of commercial laundries in the mid19th century. Many hundreds were employed at Spiers & Pond Laundry, Battersea Park Road, erected in 1879 and in the nearby London &

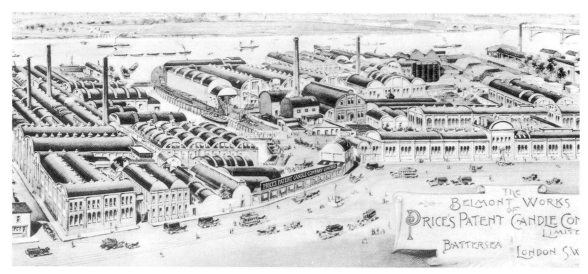

91. *A riverside view of the 1880s, showing Price's Candle Factory. In the centre is the Falcon Brook, still open to barge traffic.*

92. *(Left) A c.1912 advertisement for a more unusual product from Price's, their Bath Bouquet Toilet Soap: "A luxury at a reasonable cost".*

93. *(Above) The works of Morgan Crucible in Church Road, c.1904. These were built in 1865. To the right is the Europa public house, dating from 1844, shortly to be demolished for the 1907 extension of the factory.*

94. *The riverfront at Battersea in July 1937. Next to Battersea Bridge on the left is the LCC fire station. Morgan Crucible's buildings occupy the majority of the waterside.*

Provincial Laundry, (later called Marie Blanche Laundry), built in the 1880s, where 150 staff worked on the 1½ acre site. A matron looked after 32 younger girls living above the premises. In 1888 there were six laundries listed for this area alone.

Women also found work at May & Baker pharmaceuticals in Church Road counting and packing pills into containers and by the 20th century women could supplement their family income working at French's confectionery factory in Chatham Road, sieving and packing sweets, or else breaking up nuts for the London Nut Food Company in Battersea Park Road, or inserting lead into the products of the Royal Sovereign Pencil factory, York Road alongside the Washington Music Hall.

MANY TRADES

The Surrey Art Wallpaper Co., established in 1882, produced fine art wallpaper at their works in Battersea Park Road. Also, a paper mill on Lavender Hill was in operation until about 1922. Carlo Gatti supplied ice by the ton at their works in Parkgate Road for wet fish shops, West End restaurants and hotels.

Dawnays Ltd, founded in 1870 in Nine Elms by Sir Archibald Dawnay, Mayor of Wandsworth 1917-1919, supplied steel fabricated roofing for the super-cinemas of the 1930s including the Granada on St John's Hill, aircraft hangars and government buildings. Though originally based in Nine Elms, the company had a large works and depot in Steelworks Road, off York Road. These premises were vacated when the firm relocated to Wales. T & W Farmiloe, paint manufacturers, built a vast warehouse at Nine Elms in 1884, eventually merchandising their products as Nine Elms Paints. The warehouse was struck during the Blitz, the resulting fire being one of the most

95. *Spiers and Pond Model Laundry, at the corner of Alexandra Avenue and Battersea Park Road, c.1908.*

96. *Delivery vehicle of the London & Provincial Steam Laundry of 154 Battersea Park Road, c.1913.*

STRENGTH OF •• •• STRUCTURE

STEEL renders possible the construction of buildings such as this, forming the skeleton of the structure and carrying all main loads. Never seen in the finished building and probably never thought of by the audience it is the basis of the whole existence and safety of a modern theatre. Hidden away behind plaster and paint is 500 tons of steel varying from pieces weighing a few pounds to girders of 60 tons weight. Steel for your next contract—supplied by DAWNAYS.

spectacular in London. Paint and spirit manufacturers, with their inflammable products, are susceptible to conflagrations: the Wellington Works, Wellington Road, of Joseph Bowley, established in Battersea in 1868, contained varnish, motor spirit, naphtha, lubricating oils and paints and had its share of fires, the most severe happening in 1883 and 1906.

The Projectile & Engineering Co was one of the largest employers in Battersea. Their works in Acre Street, between Thessaly Road and Stewarts Road, manufactured pressure storage vessels, large forgings and lorry chassis frames but also a vast quantity of military shells. The bombed-out streets adjoining the factory were stacked high with shells awaiting collection during WW2. The factory only suffered a few broken windows while neighbouring streets were almost obliterated by the bombing. Post-war items were sold under the name, PECO Products. The firm was bought out by GKN and closed in 1964.

97. (Above) A 1940 advertisement for Dawnay's, structural engineers, showing steel girders destined for the Odeon, Leicester Square.

98. A c.1914 advertisement for S. Bowley's Champion motor oil. The firm was situated in the Wellington Works near Battersea Bridge.

Up and down the British Emp. :
In and out Protectorates ;
That's the way the <u>Champion</u> goes—
<u>Every drop lubricates.</u>

S. *Bowley & Son,*
Wellington Works,
Battersea Bridge, London, S.W.

99. *A steam lorry belonging to W.E. Chivers, transport contractors, based at Queen's Circus, Queenstown Road, c1923*

100. *Hibberts Ltd brought the clinker and waste from Fulham Power Station by barge to a wharf at Vicarage Crescent, where it was washed, crushed and prepared for delivery by these steam lorries to breeze block manufacturers. The product was also used for laying out athletics running tracks and speedway tracks in the 1920s and 1930s.*

THE TWENTIETH CENTURY

Industry in Battersea adapted to the 20th century mainly in the field of electrical components. The Lithanode Co. Ltd of Queenstown Road, founded in 1881, made long-life batteries for cars, lorries and buses. The Borough Council built an electrical generating station in Lombard Road by 1901 (the first Battersea Power Station). And there were dozens of small and medium sized firms engaged in manufacturing or servicing such as bakery machinery, metal working, pencil manufacture, confectionery, lift machinery, ice suppliers, pharmaceuticals, brewers, dairies etc.

An unlikely industry was that of aviation. The Short Brothers, Eustace, Horace and Oswald, rented some railway arches from the LBSCR, near Prince of Wales Circus in June 1906 to manufacture their gas-filled balloons, which were supplied from the neighbouring Field gasholder station. One of their first contracts was to construct a balloon for the Hon. Charles Rolls in which he came second in that year's Gordon Bennett Balloon race. The firm became the official aeronautical engineers to the Royal Aeronautical Club and received orders from Warwick Wright and T. O. M. Sopwith. Members' own balloons were stored in the Short Brothers' arches and the Club's own balloon could be hired at two guineas. It could be inflated and made ready for lift-off in one and a half hours, and a phone call to Battersea 788 was all that was required. In 1908 it was reported that Shorts had conducted 155 balloon ascents, carrying 483 aeronauts and had used nearly 7,000,000 cubic feet of gas.

By 1907, aircraft production was taken up by Shorts and in neighbouring arches by Howard and Warwick Wright, with some success.

Mulliner & Co. used a former roller-skating rink in Vardens Road in 1910-1911 for the construction and repair of aircraft. The works were taken over by Mrs Hilda Hewlett and Gustave Blondeau in 1912 to manufacture aircraft and supply aircraft fittings such as turnbuckles, wire strainers and a stranded cable that they only manufactured. The firm, with a staff of 25, were soon awarded contracts to build French designed Hanriots for the French and Russian governments and given work by the British to build BE2Cs. Mrs Hewlett took up residence at 34 Park Mansions, Prince of Wales Drive. The firm was restrained from expansion at its Battersea Omnia Works and moved to Bedfordshire in 1914. In December 1979, the name Hewlett House was given to a new local authority industrial development at Havelock Terrace, to commemorate Mrs Hewlett's contribution to local history

The woodworking and joinery factory of John Garlick & Sons, Candahar Road produced the framework for the wings of the Handley-Page 1500 'Berlin bomber', though assembly of the components took place at their Chelsea workshop. The super bomber was developed at the last stages of the First World War but the Armistice was signed before it became operational.

Captain W.G. Windham was a well known figure in the early days of motoring, taking part in the first London to Brighton run in 1896. He later patented the Windham Detachable Motor Body that enabled a car to be quickly converted from open tourer to town limousine. Setting up a motor body workshop at 20a-26a St John's Hill. He was one of the first to operate motor taxicabs on London's streets and undertook the testing of the mechanical knowledge of horse cab drivers at examinations held at Battersea Polytechnic. Windham founded the British Aeroplane Club in 1908 for amateur enthusiasts. While a small team were constructing aircraft in his workshop at St John's Hill, Windham built himself an aircraft on the roof of the Prince's Head public house, on the corner of Falcon Road and York Road, the *Evening News* stating that this was "one of the most novel workshops in the country". The aircraft was taken to Wembley but even after being fitted with a larger engine, could not be persuaded to leave the ground.

For one year, 1922, the Stafford motor car was produced in Battersea.

THE POWER STATION

Sir Leonard Pearce designed the interior of Battersea Power Station, and the external elevation was by Giles Gilbert Scott. Built for the London Power Co., construction began in 1929 on the site of the former Southwark and Vauxhall waterworks. The first turbine hall, the 'A' station, was completed by 1935 with the original pair of chimneys in use by 1933. The second 'B' station, commissioned in 1944, with four chimneys, was completed in 1955 and in total the station occupied a 15-acre site. A stock of 85,000 tons of coal was kept at the waterside wharf, the coal transported from the north-east coast by the generating company's own fleet of colliers. The annual consumption was in the order of 650,000 tons. The structure was listed Grade II in October 1980. The power station closed in 1983 and the generating machinery was removed. After many schemes that proved fruitless, and which have left the building roofless and derelict, Parkview International have a project for it to be converted into a major leisure complex with cinemas, theatre and exhibition floors.

NEW INDUSTRIES

Food manufacturers included the flour milling companies of Mark Mayhew and Rank-Hovis, both on the Thames-side. Next to York Place was Garton's Glucose factory, ever in trouble during the 1970s for producing a sickly sweet smell from its chimney that blew across the newly erected council flats to the east. The company spent hundreds of thousands of pounds to find a solution but closed in the late 1970s. Meux's (the 19th-century Thorne's) Brewery at Nine Elms covered a large tract of land. In York Road, S. N. Bridges & Co, better known as Stanley-Bridges, manufactured electrical tools and in nearby Lombard Road was the Walter Carson & Co. paint and varnish factory. Decca also produced radios and television sets in the borough.

The Battersea Heliport, operated by Westland Aircraft was opened on 23 April 1959 and handles over 10,000 flights per year. The helipad is used by private and commercial concerns and by the services to fly in chiefs of staff or prime ministers and foreign heads of state.

Formed in 1950 was the Birmet Television Co. of Courland Street, producing TV sets for rental through Metropolitan Relays of Lavender Hill, who had been in the area since 1929.

101. *This picture of the half-built Battersea Power Station was published in c.1934 in a booklet published by the London Power Co. Only two of the eventual four towers were built at this time (one of these first two is not visible in the darkness of this moody photograph).*

With the threat of destruction from the air in World War Two and to secure the supply of materials, many of the larger firms were to have shadow factories built elsewhere. These were on a larger scale than was possible in Battersea and many of these companies were to relocate to them during the 1960s and 1970s.

The first large-scale enterprise to close was the railway yard at Nine Elms, the steam locomotives having being removed from the Southern Region in 1967. Nine Elms gasworks closed in the 1970s and with these closures hundreds of acres were released for development. Covent Garden fruit and vegetable market relocated here in 1974. and the Royal Mail opened London's largest mail-sorting depot in Nine Elms Lane.

The riverside industries, Morgan's, Price's Candles, Manbré & Garton glucose factory (local since 1882), closed in the 1970s, taking along with them many smaller suppliers. The land released has been used for housing apartments now popular with a Thameside view.

The Local Schools

THE EARLIER SCHOOLS

A schoolmaster is mentioned in the churchwardens' accounts for 1570 but it is not clear if this denotes a local school.

Sir Walter St John's School, endowed in 1700 by the Lord of the Manor, Sir Walter St John, with the proceeds of land in Camberwell, had been in existence since at least 1668 according to the hearth tax returns of that period. The 1700 foundation deed noted that it was "to teach and instruct 20 poor boys to read, write and cast accounts". The school was rebuilt in 1859 and again in 1913-14. It closed in 1988 although the St John's trust survives as an educational charity.

Emanuel School, off Battersea Rise, was founded by Anne Sackville. In her will, proved on 6 June 1595, monies and land were left to endow and erect a hospital in Westminster, to be named Emanuel Hospital. The school remained in Westminster until 1883 when it transferred to Battersea to occupy a building first erected in 1869 as a boys' school for the Royal Victoria Patriotic Asylum, Wandsworth, that housed orphans of those killed in the Crimean War.

William Beilby's Academy in the High Street, just south of the Square, was established during the 1770s. And in 1799 the Battersea Charity School was founded in York Road.

Another early establishment was a private school run by the curate of St Mary's, the Rev. J. Gardnor, which began in the 1770s.

NATIONAL SCHOOLS

The tackling of mass illiteracy began seriously with the spread of schools related to local churches, usually under the auspices of the National Society for the Education of the Poor in the Principles of the Established Church (National schools). Alternatively, schools were provided by the British and Foreign School Society, which catered for nonconformist families. In 1814 the vicar of St Mary's founded a National school within the buildings of Sir Walter St John's School. A separate infants' and girl's school was opened in Green Lane in 1851 and enlarged in 1875 to take in the Boys' National School.

Christchurch National School was rebuilt in 1900 on the site of an earlier building founded

102. The main classrooms of Sir Walter St John's School in the High Street in 1913.

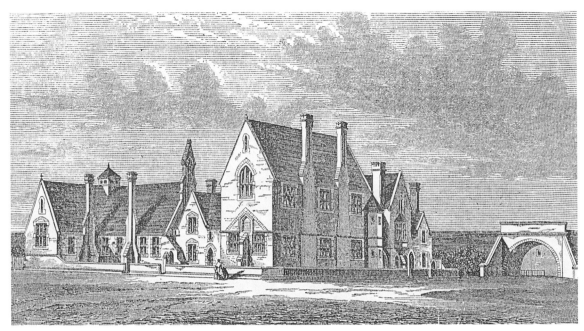

103. *St George's National Schools, New Road (later Thessaly Road), Battersea, designed by Joseph Peacock. From The Builder, 11 July 1857.*

104. *The Shrubbery, Lavender Gardens, built in 1797. This is the north elevation, built in 1843. Photograph taken c.1896 while the house was in use as Canon Clarke's school.*

in the 1850s. St John's National school, Usk Road, for boys and infants, was built in 1866 and a year later a girls' school was added nearby.

Additionally, Canon Clarke founded a girls' school in the old vicarage, near Battersea Square in 1872 just at the time when the state was making inroads into the education of the poor. Clarke's school transferred to The Shrubbery, Lavender Gardens in 1885. The School Board for London was meanwhile proceeding with its plans for their 'Towers of learning' to be constructed in all areas of the borough.

THE SCHOOL BOARD

Despite the establishment of National and British schools in Battersea they could not hope to cope with the vast increase in population too poor and often unwilling to provide their children with any kind of education. This had become a national problem and led to the passing of Forster's Education Act of 1870 which allowed for the setting up of School Boards which provided virtually free education funded by the state.

Existing provision in Battersea was surveyed by T. Paynter Allen in 1870. He correctly saw the parish as pre-eminently of the waged classes, and one in which there were pockets of overcrowding and poverty. A disproportionate rate burden fell on the small numbers of wealthy, not least by funding parish schools through the rates. In 1870, Battersea had 24 National and British schools, and some in ordinary houses. The number of places was 4,160, but average attendance was only around three-quarters of this. The cost per pupil was 32/- per annum of which 7/- came from government grants, 4/4d from voluntary contributions and 8/1d from school pence paid by parents, leaving a deficit of 2/6d. Assuming that 18% of the population was aged five-twelve, total potential demand at that time was 9,700.

Allen found 101 private schools, four of them brand new with no pupils, and seven recently closed. Setting up such establishments required "neither capital, experience, professional ability, nor special aptitude of any sort. A card placed on Saturday will raise the nucleus of a school by Monday. Many appear to have been child-minding facilities, occupying only one room, the mistresses alternating 'teaching' with mangling and shopkeeping." Allen considered that as few as twelve were really schools, although twice that number claimed to be 'select'. Attendance was irregular, averaging 1,833 per week. Charges per week ranged from 2d-1s, mostly 3d-6d. A teacher's average weekly income was 5s-6s, less than

105. Basnett Road school and St Bartholomew's church, Wycliffe Road c.1904. The building to the right is now the Greek Orthodox church of St Nectarius.

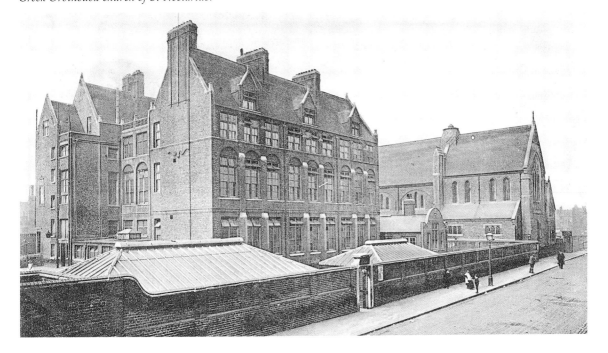

106. *Mrs Stuyers' Class II at Latchmere school, in September 1914.*

107. *Gideon Road school, c.1905.*

108. *Latchmere Road school c.1905.*

half what a washerwoman could expect to earn.

A further 700 children attended Industrial Schools in which boys were taught a craft and girls domestic duties, and 200 were educated outside Battersea. The total number at school in 1870 was about 5,900. This left 3,820 (40% of the potential number) with no school places. During the 1870s, 9,500 school-age children were added to the population, followed by 7,700 more in the 1880s. The arrival of the School Board came none too soon for Battersea.

Allen drew on a sample of two hundred households with 1,228 people, which included 546 children aged 3-14, half of them not at school. Average earnings were just £1 a week, with severe unemployment during the winter, made worse by the collapse of the building boom in 1869-70. Many households were headed by women, chiefly in laundry work, and Allen made the advanced suggestion that provision of nursery schools would release them to work more, and protect the children.

The new School Board wasted no time in identifying the size of the problem and commenced

109. *The County School for Girls in Broomwood Road c.1910.*

a building programme which lasted thirty years, providing Victorian Battersea with its most characteristic buildings. Soon, bulky three-storied blocks with large windows in a generally 'Queen Anne' style, towered above the small houses even more than did local churches and chapels. By 1900, the Board provided 25,000 places, compared with only 4,700 in church schools – hardly changed since 1870. As a result, four-fifths of local children received their education in a recently-built, well-equipped school.

These new schools were very costly, ranging from £7,000 at Bolingbroke Road in 1873, to £12,000 at Shillington Street in 1883 and almost £20,000 at Ethelburga Street in 1896. Many were soon extended. Few of the buildings were built by local firms – large-scale contractors such as Higgs of South Lambeth, Oldrey and Wall Bros., from north London were more typical. At a time when the prime cost of the average house was £150, undertaking to build a three-storey school and ancillary work required a considerable capital base.

Land costs were another significant outlay, especially in areas that had already been developed. For example, the Gideon Road site cost £3,405 and that in Holden Street £3,075 in 1876-7. Both were market garden ground five years earlier. Belleville Road, by contrast, was less built-up and the site cost only £1,661. There is no evidence that the School Board obtained land at less than the full market rate. The Board's architects E.R. Robson and Thomas Bailey were responsible in Battersea for eleven and seven new schools, respectively.

By 1900, many Board Schools accommodated in excess of 1,200 pupils (1,840 at Latchmere and 1,616 at Shillington Street). The numbers are difficult to envisage nowadays, although it should be remembered that with few exceptions, they provided education from the ages of five to thirteen. Overall, the number of children at school in 1904 represented about 18% of the population, identical to Allen's 1870 estimate.

With so many Board Schools, it is possible only to present a brief sample of the riches contained in the London Metropolitan Archives. Bolingbroke Road school opened its doors on 1 December 1873, the first to be completed in Battersea. It was built by John Spink of Clapham Junction for £5,400 in a remarkable seven months, on a site which had somehow escaped the attention of a builder. The school had to be extended in 1880. In 1877 there were 792 pupils, paying 2d per week (free

education did not come until 1891). A Mr Pink was the boys' headmaster, and his wife was in charge of infants, while the girls were under Miss Adeline Deacon. Very few of the initial recruits had ever attended school before, and did so rather erratically, the fee no doubt being a problem for many families. After two months, 239 infants were enrolled, but average attendance was only 171, reduced dramatically in February 1874 by an outbreak of measles. Mrs Pink was assisted by four 'pupil teachers', teenagers learning the job in the most practical way, and paid the niggardly sum of four shillings per week. The vicar, Erskine Clarke, and the head of Morgan Crucible were frequent visitors. The winter of 1881 was very severe, and despite its location, only four children attended on 20 January!

Most of the first intake of boys were "very backward and illiterate", and within two weeks there were problems with bad language and assaults, including one on a master – Mr Pink had two assistants and three pupil teachers for 240 boys. The logistics of taking one hundred boys to London Zoo in September 1876 are difficult to imagine. At the girls' school, opened in January 1874, the standards were as low as the boys', as was the discipline. In January 1877 there were outbreaks of scarlet fever and smallpox. At that time, there were five staff, a ratio of one to fifty girls. In order to fit them for their future role, small groups of older girls were attending the cookery centre at Mantua Street school by the mid-1880s.

The second Board School in Battersea opened in Winstanley Road in January 1874. It was built by George Stephenson of Chelsea for £5,900, while the site cost almost £4,000, reflecting the tremendous upsurge in values here in the 1860s. The management committee was chaired by the Vicar of St Peter's, and consisted of a mixture of tradesmen (bookseller, draper), the middle class (a gentleman, bank manager), along with Mrs Byers and Mrs Millar – the School Board being one of the few bodies offering a public role to women at that time. They were not at all representative of the parents of pupils, who were almost exclusively working-class: engine drivers, candle factory foremen, charladies and labourers, etc. In 1877, fees were a flat 3d per week. An Inspector's report of the time shows better standards and discipline than at Bolingbroke Road, although the Infants' was "too noisy" and overcrowded. Two pupil teachers were sacked for poor examination results.

On 20 July 1877, the log reports the breakdown of Miss Robinson's health after only two weeks in the girls' school! Six months later we learn that Mr Stonehouse had 'kept' 13/6d in fees, which were to be deducted from his salary – apparently absent-minded rather than dishonest. The school seems to have been hastily built, for in 1877 there were problems with light, heat and leaks. Corporal punishment was evidently very common, with over two hundred cases of boys in Lower II suffering punishment in October 1877. At that time, there were 1,204 pupils registered in accommodation for only 1,076. The headmaster was paid £150 p.a., not much more than the best-paid skilled workers whose children he taught. As at Bolingbroke Road, attendance by girls was lower than boys and infants, probably because they were kept at home to assist with running the family, or even earning at some domestic trade such as laundering or sewing.

By the time of the 1880 inspection, work was said to be "too mechanical, with too much briskness, too little cheerfulness". Some teachers were criticised for putting "no life into teaching, and [are] harsh towards the children". Once again the girls' school had problems, when in October 1881 Miss Douglas "withdrew" after only two days, as "she was not strong enough for the post." Overcrowding continued into the late 1880s, as delays were encountered in building Plough Lane school, despite the close proximity of Mantua Street school, but by 1895, the district had its full complement of places.

SOME PRIVATE SCHOOLS

Despite the growing popularity of the Board Schools some small private enterprises were still to be found. Local directories for 1891 list 26 'schools', located in ordinary dwelling houses, mostly small terraced properties. Only two were run by men – Thomas Montelli's preparatory school at 43 Bennerley Road and that of the Rev. J. Parr, Halbrake School at 21-3 Park Road, New Wandsworth. The rest were run by women, virtually all spinsters. Ten were for 'ladies', two for 'girls' and four were 'preparatory'. Sixteen of these establishments were located in or to the south of Lavender Hill-St John's Hill, and there were none in the typically working-class streets of north Battersea except Miss E. Adams' ladies' school (54 Cabul Road) and Mrs Mary Hannington's (114 New Road, now Thessaly Road). It is unlikely that these schools taught more than 20-30 pupils on average, providing in total less than half of one typical board school.

On a much larger scale, the Royal Freemasons' Girls' School moved to Battersea in 1852, to a red-brick Gothic building designed by Philip Hardwick. It contained 160 girls and continued in use until 1932. The girls were removed to Rickmansworth, Herts in 1934 and the school demolished. The Peabody Estate in Boutflower Road was built on the site.

Battersea Grammar School, St John's Hill was founded in 1875 as an offshoot of Sir Walter St John's School. When it moved to Streatham in 1936 the St John's Hill site was used for construction of the Granada Cinema.

110. The senior school of the Freemasons' Girls' School in Boutflower Road c.1910. The junior school was at Weybridge, Surrey.

111. Battersea Grammar on St John's Hill, c.1904. The building was demolished 1934/5 and replaced by the Granada cinema.

112 & 113. *Two views of the Battersea Polytechnic. Above is the Great Hall, in use for concerts and lectures, c.1905. Below is the Electrical Workshop, in 1905.*

THE POLYTECHNIC

The Polytechnic in Battersea Park Road was opened in February 1894 by the Prince of Wales. Holloway Brothers of Battersea erected the building, which cost £60,000, on part of the site of the Albert Palace. The efforts of the people of Battersea managed to raise £6,164 16s 1d of the building costs. The Polytechnic was later called the Battersea College of Technology. In 1966 it became the University of Surrey and two years later part of Westminster College. The designer of the 1959 Austin Mini, Alec Issigonis was a former student here.

TEACHER TRAINING

St John's College for training school masters was founded in 1840. Battersea House was chosen as the principal's house and later an extensive range of classrooms and facilities was added, sharing them with Sir Walter St John's school. The college amalgamated with St Mark's, Chelsea in 1925 and the site, except Battersea House, was built on by the Council. The St John's housing estate was not fully occupied until 1934.

Southlands College in the High Street, a Wesleyan teacher training college for women students, opened in 1872 in the former home of General George Pollock, a veteran of the Indian and Afghan wars. He had renamed the house Southlands in 1850, dispensing with its original name of The Retreat as this, perhaps, impugned his own military career. The premises held 146 young ladies in residence. The College moved to Southfields in 1927/8.

115. The hallway and main staircase of Battersea House when in use as the Principal's house at St John's College, c.1908.

114. St John's College. The Principal's house, later to be renamed Battersea House, is dated 1699. The photograph was taken c.1908.

116. Southlands College in the High Street, c.1919. The house was built for the Duchess of Angouleme during the French Revolution and was known as The Retreat. It later became home to Field Marshal Sir George Pollock, who renamed it Southlands. The building was largely destroyed during bombing in 1940.

117. The students' day room at Southlands College, c.1905.

118. A scene at Battersea Dogs' Home in the 1920s.

A Dog's best friend

Battersea is nowadays famous for its Dogs' Home, which arrived in its remote and soundproof site by the Thames in 1871.

It had been founded by Mary Tealby on 2 October 1860 in Holloway as the Temporary Home for Lost and Starving Dogs. Today, its old site there is appropriately used as an urban farm.

In 1871 the Home moved to Battersea Park Road. When first founded it housed 21,000 to 28,000 stray dogs each year and by 1896 the numbers had increased to 46,000, but then fell to 8 to 12,000 after the Second World War. In 2001 it looked after just under 10,000 dogs. It was estimated that in the first hundred years of operation over 2,000,000 dogs passed through its doors.

Many people do not realise that the Home also looks after stray cats. They were probably included at Holloway but a formal motion to take in cats was passed in 1883 when funding was found for 210 strays. Two years later a cattery was built. In 2001 the Home took in over 3,000 cats.

The Dogs' Home is responsible for collecting stray dogs from police stations throughout the London area within the M25 orbital motorway, and the animals are kept for seven days to enable owners to reclaim them, before being offered to the general public for adoption. Since 1954 the Home has been able to find homes for almost every fit dog brought into its care. In 1991 the Queen opened a £3 million four-storey block containing 117 kennels named Tealby Kennels. In 1996, £6 million was expended on the Kent Kennels, with 164 kennels named after the Home's President, Prince Michael of Kent.

THE DOG STATUE

The anti-vivisection cause was strong in Battersea. A private house was converted into a hospital (for humans) in 1902, largely due to the generosity of Elizabeth, Lady Headley. She was a firm protagonist of saving animals from medical experiments and she named her building the Anti-Vivisection Hospital; this later became the Battersea General Hospital, which closed in 1974 and was demolished.

119. The Anti-vivisection and Battersea General Hospital, Albert Bridge Road, c.1906.

The existence of the Hospital was possibly why a celebrated anti-vivisection dispute arose in Battersea in 1907. In 1905 the Borough Council had accepted, as a gift from the International Anti-Vivisection Council, a statue of a dog, to be erected on the newly-opened Latchmere recreation ground. The mayor unveiled it on 15 September 1906. The provocative inscription read: 'In memory of the Brown Terrier Dog Done to Death in the laboratories of University College in February, 1903, after having endured Vivisection extending over Two months and having been handed over from one Vivisector to Another Till Death came to his Release'.

A carnival held in the autumn of 1907, to gather funds for the Anti-Vivisection Hospital, brought further attention to Battersea and to the existence of the statue. On 20 November that year students from University College and Middlesex Hospital attacked the memorial, one with a sledgehammer, almost severing it from the base. Ten students were arrested and fined £5 each, but more attacks followed and the police were detailed to mount a guard day and night in two huts provided for them as shelter. The Council elections of 1909 saw a change in politics and at a council meeting on 8 March 1911 it was decided to destroy the memorial and the inscription. The statue was duly removed and the results of the scrap metal amounted to 30s.

120. The Little Brown Dog Statue in Latchemere Recreation Ground c.1910.

Leisurely Times

PUBLIC HOUSES

Early references to drinking establishments are in the churchwardens' accounts for 1645 when a brewhouse at Nine Elms is mentioned and in 1651 when "Scales and weights for the Ayle tasters were provided". Rowdiness and drunkenness were implied at a public meeting in 1653 when the constables and churchwardens "certified who were fit and who were to be suppressed of the alehouse keepers".

The 17th-century lists include only four pubs: the Mermayd 1636, the Cocke 1639, the Plough 1681 and the Starr 1684. Although the Castle is first mentioned in 1702 and the Raven in 1765, both probably date from the 1660s. By the 18th century a further fourteen establishments are mentioned, among them the Falcon and the Nag's Head in York Road (demolished about 1980).

The churchwardens' annual dinners became ever more expensive: that at the Castle in 1770

122. The Castle Inn in the High Street, 1868.

121. The Plough Inn, St John's Hill, in 1867.

123. *The Raven inn, Battersea Square, in 1876. Notice the village pump (see also ill. 22).*

124. *The White Hart in Lombard Road, in 1868. Access was available directly from the Thames.*

125. The Prince's Head in York Road in 1879.

cost £5, at the Raven in 1770 another £5 and £9. 5s at 'the Faulcon' in 1767. The notorious Red House on the riverside was said to date from the 1720s. By the 1840s it could attract up to 50,000 people a day to attend the pigeon shoots and fairground. Another attraction was the flounders breakfast, which was served at 10 each day. The Rev. Thomas Kirk witnessed an Easter fair here and fulminated from his pulpit "Surely if there was a place out of hell which surpassed Sodom and Gomorrah in ungodliness and abomination this was it." On a Sunday he saw from 60 to 120 horses and donkeys racing, foot racing, walking matches, flying boats, roundabouts, comic actors, conjurers, shameless dancers, fortune tellers, gamblers of every description, beggars, drinking booths and innumerable stalls for hawkers.

The White Hart in Lombard Road dated from 1757 and the Duchess of York, Battersea Park Road appeared in 1792. Near the Red House was The Old House at Home, a thatched farmhouse with a beerhouse attached that became famous for its egg flip of hot ale, eggs and sugar supplied

to early morning revellers on their way to the Red House.

The Falcon was the scene of revelry in the early 19th century when funeral parties halted at the inn for refreshments and matters could get out of hand. The publican's name in about 1800 was Robert Death and the artist John Nixon happened upon one of these scenes of merriment and sketched the celebrants. This was soon published as the undertakers at 'Death's Door' *(ill. 126).* Most of the public houses were rebuilt in the 1880s and 1890s but the Raven can be said now to be the oldest surviving. The third longest-named pub in Britain was the London, Chatham and Dover Railway Tavern in Cabul Road.

The building development of the 19th century saw a proliferation of public houses, beer shops and beerhouses. The totals for the parish were 62 in 1852, 75 by 1862 and 155 in 1871. Many of the beer shops and beerhouses remained unnamed but added to the 93 named pubs and other drinking places in 1891/2 we have a total of 207. Battersea Park Road alone had 16 by the 1860s, almost on every corner, and Chatham Road had

126. 'Undertakers at Death's Door' at the Falcon Inn, drawn by John Nixon and published in 1801. (See p.105.)

no less than five public houses at that time.

The late 20th century has seen some pubs close, converted for residential use or else become wine bars, though in the former Hastings furnishing store in Falcon Road a Yates Wine Lodge opened on its ground floor in about 2000. Historical associations are often lost with the current trend for renaming: the Craven Hotel on Lavender Hill is now called Harvey's and the Clockhouse in

Battersea Park Road was renamed the Bar Room Bar about 1998, but an interesting addition is the Asparagus public house opened on 26 July 1998 at the corner of Falcon Road and Battersea Park Road.

ENTERTAINMENTS

Early forms of entertainment were provided in the 18th and 19th centuries by the Red House and the nearby Flora Tea Gardens and Tivoli Gardens. The Albert Palace in Prince of Wales Drive was originally built for the Dublin Exhibition of 1872 and re-erected here substantially enlarged. It specialised in high-class musical entertainment and possessed an art gallery. It was licensed for entertainment from only 1884 to 1887 in its Connaught Hall, the nave and also an attached outdoor theatre that backed onto Battersea Park Road. The controlling company collapsed in 1886, after which the grounds and building changed ownership but, still proving a complete financial failure, was demolished about 1894. Battersea Polytechnic and some of the Mansions in Prince of Wales Drive were built on its site.

Many of the public houses had music halls attached, some no more than a room divided off

127. The Red House c.1800. An isolated, and at times notorious inn on the banks of the Thames near to the present Chelsea Bridge. It derived its name from being built of red bricks.

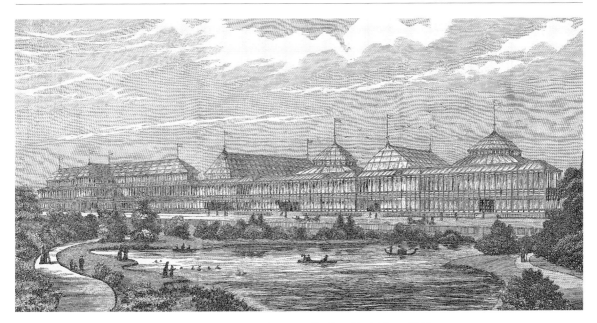

128. *The Albert Palace and the lake in Battersea Park. From The Graphic 28 June 1884.*

for the purpose, but they all had to have a licence. The Royal Standard in York Road was licensed from 1886 to 1917, undergoing nine name changes, amongst them, the Washington Music Hall and the Palace of Varieties; later it became a cinema. Three public houses in Battersea Park Road had music halls, the Commercial, the Park, and the Magpie, also called the Battersea Music Hall and the Palace of Varieties. The Corunna Music Hall, attached to the General Moore public house, Stewarts Road, licensed from 1869 to 1889, measured only 29' 6" by 19' 6".

Other music halls were at the Crown public house on Lavender Hill, 1870 to 1875, and the Queen Victoria on Falcon Road 1868 to 1885.

The St Mary's Temperance Hall and Green Lane school (about 1880) had a capacity of 430. This was in use for concerts on Mondays and Saturdays and at other times it was a dancing academy.

Many of the public house music halls were closed by the Metropolitan Board of Works Act of 1878 which was concerned with safety, fire regulations and evacuation of premises, and inspections after 1880 led to many licences being revoked or refused. This led to more purpose-built premises being opened.

129. *The transept of the Albert Palace.*

130. *Pigeon shooting at the Red House c.1829. Members of the Red House Club shooting for the Gold Cup.*

131. Scene from the 'Indian village' at the Albert Palace in 1885.

NEW THEATRES

The Queen's Theatre in Prairie Street, with an entrance also from Queenstown Road, was erected in 1884 as the Park Town Hall and Theatre, a community hall for the Park Town estate tenants. It was licensed for entertainment from 1890 to 1897 as the Park Town Theatre of Varieties and the Queen's Theatre. The building survives as a private residence and a storage warehouse.

The Shakespeare on Lavender Hill opened in 1896 and saw the acting talents of Ellen Terry, Lillie Langtry and Sarah Bernhardt. The theatre was converted to cinema use in 1923 but was bombed in the last war and demolished in 1957.

The piano makers, Munts Brothers, in St John's Hill, opened up part of their premises in 1890 for high-class concerts but on applying for a licence were refused unless improvements were made. After rebuilding it was reopened in 1894 as the Grand Hall of Varieties. Overwhelmed by the competition of the New Grand, also on St John's Hill in 1900, the hall was little used until conversion in 1914 to the Imperial Cinema with 800 seats, renamed the Ruby in the 1960s, after the then owner's wife's name. It was demolished about 1985.

The Grand Theatre (formerly New Grand), was

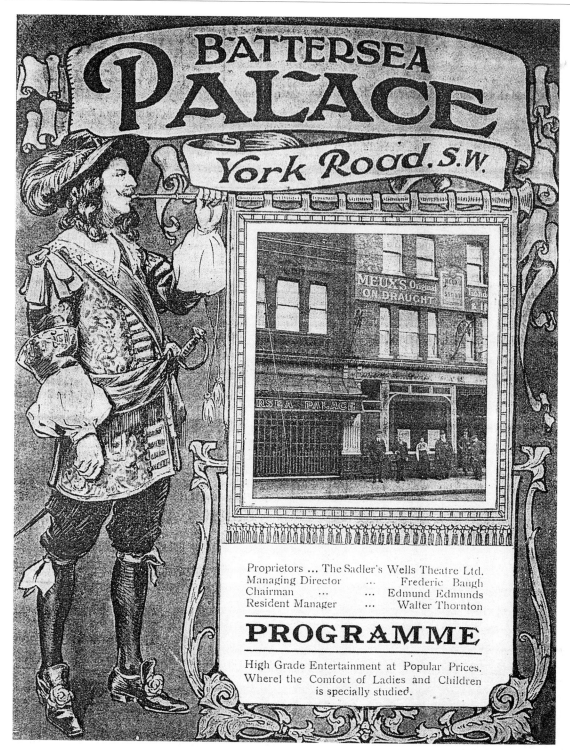

132. *Programme for the Palace Theatre (previously the Washington Music Hall), York Road, c.1908.*

133. *Interior of the Washington Music Hall, York Road, 1886.*

134. *The 'Female Blondin' crossing the Thames on a tightrope from Battersea to Cremorne Gardens, Chelsea, depicted in the Illustrated London News 24 August, 1861.*

135. The Shakespeare Theatre, Lavender Hill, c.1910.

mainly financed by the music hall artist and pantomime dame, Dan Leno, who lived nearby in Clapham Park. Artists appearing here included Marie Lloyd, Little Titch and Harry Tate. The theatre was used as a cinema in the 1920s, eventually becoming the Essoldo cinema and from 1963 to 1983, a bingo club, and it is now used for rock concerts.

CINEMAS

The earliest cinema in Battersea was probably the Bio Picture Palace in Northcote Road, opening in 1908, using a former assembly room. It was successively called the Bolingbroke Picture Hall, the Globe and lastly the Century, closing in the 1960s before conversion into a supermarket. The Biograph, St John's Road, opened in 1909, and by 1914 there were twelve cinemas in Battersea including, the Gem on Lavender Hill, the Brighton in Battersea Park Road, the Cinema de Luxe in Plough Road, the Electroscope, Falcon Road, the Globe, Lavender Hill, the Radium, York Road, the Surrey Bioscope, Battersea Park Road, the Queen's Cinema, Queenstown Road and the Empire on St John's Hill. Many of these were no more than converted shops with as few as 200 seats and were to close as purpose-built cinemas were built. The Pavilion on Lavender Hill opened in 1916 and the Super Palace, with 1,200 seats (formerly the Washington Music Hall) was opened in 1924.

The largest Battersea cinema was the Granada on St John's Hill with 3,001 seats; opened in 1937, it was converted to a bingo club in the 1980s and closed in 1997. The building remains empty.

136. George Carroll as Baron and William P. Sheen as Baroness in a performance of Cinderella at the Shakespeare Theatre in 1907-8.

SPORTING PEOPLE

The first Thames regatta took place in 1775 at Battersea when thousands of spectators lined the banks. The Doggett's Coat and Badge races for watermen finished at Cadogan Pier near the Albert Bridge.

The Red House on the Thames waterfront was famous for the bird shooting contests, dog fights, prize fights, donkey races and the associated gambling. This was finally put a stop to in 1852.

The land around the Red House was used for several duels, the most famous being that between the Duke of Wellington and Lord Winchelsea on 21 March 1829. The Roman Catholic Relief Act was in process through parliament, guided by the Duke who had to deal with vehement Protestant opposition from clergy, the press

137. *The Grand Theatre, St John's Hill, c.1904. Opened in 1900, it has also been used for cinema performances as the Essoldo, and afterwards as a bingo hall. It is now in use as a rock performing venue.*

138. *The Pavilion cinema, Lavender Hill, c.1926. Opened in 1916, it was destroyed by a VI flying bomb on 17 August 1944, together with the parade of shops on the left, killing 28 people.*

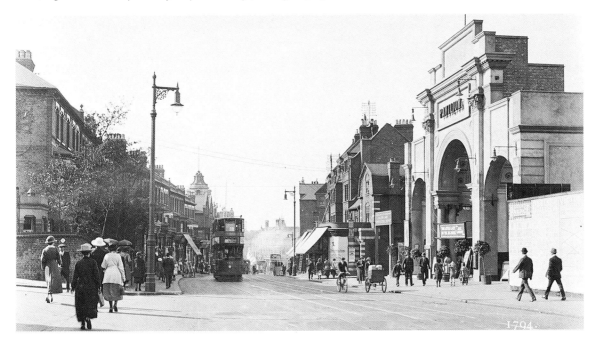

139. *The Granada cinema, St John's Hill, in 1939.*

140. *The duel between the Duke of Wellington and Lord Winchelsea. The Duke is depicted as a lobster claw, alluding to the nickname given to British troops because of their red tunics. He is also wearing a monk's robe and rosary to indicate his support of Roman Catholic emancipation. Caricature by William Heath, published March 1829. (See p. 112)*

141. Advertisement for the grand opening of the Battersea Stadium Wrestling Club, 19 April 1936, held at the Greyhound Racing Track, Lombard Road, near the railway bridge.

and Tories. Lord Winchelsea accused the Duke, amongst other things, of introducing Popery into every department of State. Neither opponent aimed to strike a hit and the duel finished with an apology accepted by the Duke.

Bowling alleys and greens were available at public houses such as the Prodigal's Return and many of the pubs had their snooker and billiards saloons.

Swimming took place at the Latchmere baths, opened in 1889; a gymnasium was added in 1899 with billiards and bagatelle an added attraction in 1901. Nine Elms Baths opened in 1901.

A roller skating rink was opened in Vardens Road, in the 1880s-90s, much later in use as a snooker hall.

A Temperance billiard and snooker hall was opened on Battersea Rise (*c*1910), ironically be-

coming a public house about 1997.

The Battersea Amateur Boxing Association hold their tournaments at Battersea Town Hall.

Due to lack of space within this built-up suburban area, most sporting events have taken place either in Battersea Park or on Clapham Common. The Clapham Common Golf Club, founded in 1873, used the northern side of the Common until 1939. Early morning play was instituted in 1905 as the Council considered play at other times a danger to the public.

The Battersea Cricket Club was formed in 1856 using the Prince Albert public house as its headquarters and Battersea Park for its matches. Two Battersea cricketers, Laurence B. Fishlock and John F. Parker, played for Surrey in the period 1930s to 1950s, Fishlock scoring over 25,000 runs from 1931 to 1952. A team from Price's Candles played against a Christian Socialist team in the 1840s. The firm had encouraged its workers to take up sport.

Prior to the founding of the Amateur Athletic Association in 1880 the sport was termed 'pedestrianism' and walking, running and hopping competitions were held on a track in Falcon Lane and on another near the Red House in Battersea Fields and on Clapham Common. Against the railway embankment in Green Lane (renamed Vicarage Crescent) was the Star Athletic Grounds, in use about 1890.

Battersea Park became the fashionable rendezvous for the new cycling craze in the 1880s and 1890s. The Pioneer Cycling Club was founded in 1881 with local Clapham MP Percy Thornton a member; the club began continental touring in 1889. Other cycling clubs by 1912 were the South London Clarion Cycling Club, the St Mark's, based at the church on Battersea Rise and also the Amalgamated Society of Engineers, Battersea branch.

An unusual sport, held on Boxing Day just before and after the Great War, was the coalmen's race carrying 1cwt of coal from the Plough at Clapham to the Rising Sun on Battersea Rise near St Mark's church. Due to increased traffic the race was transferred to the drill hall parade ground on St John's Hill.

In the 1920s the London County Council built a 3-lap to 1-mile track in Battersea Park almost upon the site of the 1850s track. The track was relaid as an all-weather surface in 1983 with six lanes of 400 metres. The interior field caters for all throwing and jumping events.

Town Services

The first Vestry Hall was built with funds given by the government as compensation for losing grazing rights when Battersea Park was opened in 1858. Lammas Hall, as it was called, stood on the corner of Surrey Lane and Westbridge Road

In 1888 Battersea vestry obtained a separate existence from the Wandsworth District Board of Works and, full of radical and enthusiastic members, proceeded to improve the amenities available to residents. It took over the Board of Works premises on Battersea Rise as offices and administrative headquarters.

The Vestry became a Borough Council in 1900, and it was enthused with the promotion of direct labour for building projects, particularly those which improved housing and social conditions in Battersea. The Council was soon involved in building housing, baths and libraries.

143. *Lammas Hall at the Surrey Lane junction with Westbridge Road, c.1962.*

142. *Steam rollers in action laying a new road surface in Northcote Road c.1890.*

144. The ladies' pool at the Latchmere Road swimming baths c.1930.

PUBLIC BATHS AND LIBRARIES

Even as a vestry Battersea had been eager to
provide public baths. The foundation stone of
Latchmere Baths had been laid in 1888 and they
were opened in 1889. They originally contained
3 swimming baths, 81 slipper baths, a public
washhouse, which was then the largest in London, together with public halls and meeting
rooms.

Nine Elms Baths, built in 1899-1901, had one
swimming pool – the largest covered pool in
Britain at the time – 50 slipper baths, a public
washhouse and a laundry. The swimming pool
could be covered with a floor and the space
converted into a public hall for nearly 1,500 people.

Bathing facilities were also provided at the
Plough Road Institute and Museum. Here, 36
slipper baths were installed in a building which
also contained a billiards room and a gymnasium. A wash house was installed at Southlands
House in the High Street, when taken over by the
Council in 1929 after Southlands School moved
to Southfields.

The first local public lending library was opened
at Lammas Hall in Westbridge Road in 1888 until
its transfer to the Southlands branch library in
1928.

*145. Latchmere Road baths, decorated for the Silver
Jubilee of King George V, 1935.*

146. *(Above) Testing the steel roof trusses of the Nine Elms swimming baths c.1890.*

147. *(Below) Plough Road Institute, Museum and Baths, at the corner of Plough Road and Benham Street, March 1968.*

148. *(Bottom right) The Central Library, Lavender Hill, c.1914.*

The Central Library on Lavender Hill opened in March 1890 together with a branch in Lurline Gardens. The Reference Library in Altenburg Gardens, built by direct labour, was opened in 1925. Two shops were converted for use to form the Northcote Road branch in 1948; this has since been rebuilt.

Battersea Park Road library has replaced the Lurline Gardens branch library.

A NEW TOWN HALL

Lord Rosebery opened the Town Hall on Lavender Hill, on 15 November 1893. Designed by Edward Mountford, architect of the Battersea Polytechnic and of the central library on Lavender Hill. The Hall was in use for concerts, exhibitions, political rallies, picture shows, ballroom dancing, boxing tournaments and home to many other cultural activities. It became redundant on amalgamation of the Borough with Wandsworth in 1965 but has been revived as the Battersea Arts Centre, in the vanguard of new theatrical productions and art forms and home to a puppet theatre.

The Electricity Generating Station, Lombard Road, was built by the works department and opened 1901. The Council also built Electric House, Lavender Hill, which contained the offices and showrooms of the Council's electricity department, opened by the Mayor, Jimmy Lane in 1927. Demonstrations and classes were held each week to train housewives and those wishing to convert from other power sources, in ironing, vacuuming, cooking and even how to boil a kettle with the new electrical appliances.

The Council opened an Infants' milk depot, York Road in 1902, and was the first London borough to set up a health visiting service in 1908. It also established a maternity and child welfare centre in 1917 and took over a tuberculosis dispensary in Battersea Park Road in 1921.

The churchyard at St Mary's was closed to new burials in 1853 and the vestry purchased 7 ½ acres on Battersea Rise for a new cemetery. This was far too small to cater for a fast-growing area and was full by 1885; in 1891 a new Battersea cemetery, covering almost 125 acres, was opened in Morden.

HOUSING THE POOR

The St John's almshouses, first mentioned in 1675, stood on Battersea Park Road (near the site of Christchurch), and the inmates were referred to

149. Battersea Town Hall. .

150. *The old workhouse in Battersea Square in 1844, shortly before demolition.*

as "Ye poor people at Ye gate". Sir Walter St John placed the half-dozen cottages at the disposal of the churchwardens for the "very antient, past labour, bed ridden and lame" of the village, at the nominal rent of 10s per annum. The overseers added a further six rooms in 1721 at a cost of £117 2s 7d. These almshouses remained in use until about 1834/5.

Jane Morland was the first "Misteris" of the Workhouse in Battersea Square, which was opened in 1733. Additionally, Dovedale Cottages in Battersea Park Road to the east of St Stephen's church, were funded in the 19th century by a bequest of Mrs Lightfoot of Balham. There are 12 apartments and a small chapel.

HOSPITALS

Canon Clarke instigated the purchase in 1876, and the alterations at a cost of £6.000, of Bolingbroke House as a hospital. The first patient was admitted in 1880 to 'The Bolingbroke Self-Supporting Hospital and House in Sickness'. Further additions to the hospital were made in 1927 and 1936, the old house being demolished in 1937.

In the south-west corner of the Borough stood St James's Hospital, opened in 1910 by John Burns, as an LCC general hospital once containing 903 beds. This was closed in the 1970s.

151. *Bolingbroke Hospital, Bolingbroke Grove c.1934. In the background is Bolingbroke House, the original hospital, shortly to be demolished.*

152. Bolingbroke House, the seat of William Willis Esq, c.1830. It was converted into Bolingbroke Hospital by Canon Clarke. The house was one of the five houses of Five Houses Lane, later renamed Bolingbroke Grove.

The Wandsworth and Clapham Union Workhouse on St John's Hill was opened in 1838 to house paupers under the Poor Law Reform Act of 1834. The infirmary was added in 1870. When the workhouse moved to Swaffield Road in 1886 the infirmary was renamed St John's Hospital and contained 637 beds. The hospital closed in the 1970s, though parts of the building remain, converted into flats.

KEEPING THE PEACE
The Constables for Battersea are mentioned in 1560 with responsibilities for maintaining the peace, guarding the church when necessary and keeping in repair the stocks and fire buckets. The town stocks, in the Square in 1662, were moved to the church gate in 1811. The only mention of their use is of some boys placed in them in 1821. The watch house, where felons could be detained overnight, was removed from the Square in 1772 to Battersea Park Road near to where Christchurch was built. Crime seems to have been a small scale problem, Ralph Blundall was fined £5 in 1729 for poaching hares and in 1801 John Davis, the watchman on Battersea Bridge, was given £2 12s 6d for apprehending a turkey thief.

An early reference to murder in Battersea is from a statement in the Pleas to the Crown, before the King's Justices at Bermondsey, in the reign of King Henry III (1216-1227):

"Thomas the vintner was found dead in his bed at Batrichse, and John of St Albans who was his servant is suspect of that death, and therefore let him be put in exigent and outlawed. He was not a-tithing and had no chattels".

The term 'exigent' meant that the accused had not appeared at court and was therefore an outlaw; not a 'tithing' meant that ten men could not vouch for his good behaviour.

Of some notoriety was the murder of Mrs Sarah Eleanor Macfarlane on 29 April 1844, on Battersea Bridge by Augustus Dalmas *(ill. 154)*. She was buried at St Mary's but Dalmas escaped the hangman's noose, being transported to Australia.

The Metropolitan Police built police stations in Battersea Bridge Road, Battersea Park Road (opposite Notre Dame convent) and on Lavender Hill in 1892 with the South-western Magistrates Court attached. The courthouse, empty from 1939, was rebuilt with the police station in 1963.

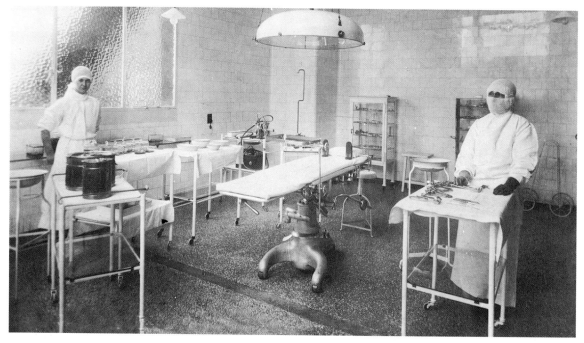

153. *The main operating room at Bolingbroke Hospital c.1930.*

154. *Augustus Dalmas committing the murder of Sarah McFarlane on Battersea Bridge on 29 April 1844 (See p. 121).*

155. *The police station, Battersea Bridge Road, c.1914.*

156. *View from the roof of 217 Lavender Hill showing the new police station and magistrates court, 1963.*

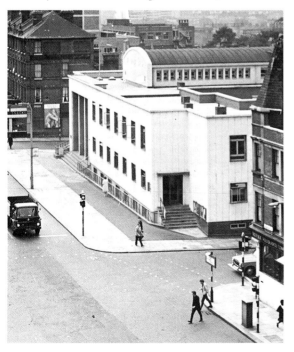

FIRE FIGHTING

Fire fighting in Battersea is mentioned in a church inventory of 1595 that listed "a long ladder, twelve bucketts, a great iron hooke and two ropes for the hooke" – the iron hooks were attached to long poles for removing burning thatch from buildings. The leather buckets were replaced in 1777 with three engines for £3, probably simple hand pumps.

The railway companies had their own fire engines at Nine Elms works by 1880, installing 120 hydrants, but employing the firemen only at night. By 1897 the LCC had three fire stations with fire floats on the Thames, including the station built to the west of Battersea Bridge, designated 'Gamma': this was changed to 'K23' in 1965. The Metropolitan Fire Brigade station on the corner of Battersea Park Road and Simpson Street was built in 1873-4. The LCC station in Northcote Road was built in 1907 but abandoned by 1914 no doubt due to mechanisation of the appliances. The Este Road station has replaced the Battersea Park Road station, badly damaged in a 1944 rocket attack.

157. *A Metropolitan Fire Brigade horse-drawn escape, in Simpson Street, c.1908.*

158. *Metropolitan Fire Brigade station at the corner of Battersea Park Road and Simpson Street, c.1908.*

159. *The LCC Fire Brigade station at Northcote Road, c.1906. It was built that year, closed by 1913-14, and demolished c.1970*

Political Life

The arrival of the railway companies in the period 1838 to 1865 brought about a revolution in housing and social conditions, the population increasing from 19,600 in 1861 to 54,016 within ten years. Empty housing in Battersea and elsewhere was blamed on the high fares into London, which brought about the Cheap Trains Act of 1883, enabling workers to catch an early morning 'workmen's train'.

Railway employment was organised so that it was possible to rise through the ranks in status and pay. Between 1856 and 1861, sixty of the station masters employed by the London Brighton & South Coast Railway had progressed from the following trades: porters 18, policemen 14, clerks 12, and gatekeepers 5.

Discipline was severe, with the LBSC dismissing a booking clerk in 1872 for not accounting for excess fares; another was cautioned for providing a passenger with incorrect information. A porter was sacked for unapproved absence and another porter was fined for damaging a passenger's luggage. The railway companies provided a wide range of benefit societies to cater for workers' sickness, injury, superannuation, and widows' and orphans' funding.

Porters at the Nine Elms depot of the London & South Western Railway had sought in 1845 a reduction in their 16-hour day at a rate of 18- to 20/- per week. The company organised a new agreement and dismissed 39 of those who refused to sign.

The railway staff had, from the 1860s, called for a reduction in hours and/or overtime payments in petitions and walkouts, but were not fully established as trade unions until the 1870s. The engine drivers of the LSWR won a reduction in 1875 from 12 to 10 hours per day. Battersea railwaymen were strong supporters of the formation of the Amalgamated Society of Railway Servants in 1871, later renamed the National Union of Railwaymen.

The Amalgamated Society of Engineers went on strike at the London Chatham & Dover Railway works in Battersea in 1874. A leading activist in the strike was Thomas Atkinson, who had been a rivet boy at George Stephenson's locomotive works in 1824 and an apprentice in the fitting shop from 1825 to1830, working on the 'Rocket'. A Grand Concert was held in his honour at

160. *Members of the Nine Elms no. 2 branch of the National Union of Railwaymen hold their banner aloft in 1916.*

Battersea Town Hall to raise money for him.

Railway accidents are reported in many deaths and injuries. George Smith, carriage cleaner was run over by a train in 1871, Frank Newton, a shunter was coupling wagons at Nine Elms when his foot became stuck in some points and he too was killed by a passing train. Working on the railway was considered a dangerous occupation. Between 1901 and 1911, 5508 people were killed and 238,708 injured throughout Britain.

Working-class organisation developed in Battersea in the 1870s and 1880s through the strength of trade unionism, the co-operative movement and friendly societies. The Railway Orphans' Fund Fête, held on 14 September 1885 at the Albert Palace, was attended by an estimated 10,000 people.

A major change in the composition of the area's railway community took place between 1908 and 1910 when the LSWR moved its engineering works from Nine Elms to Eastleigh in Hampshire – the carriage and wagon works had moved there in 1891. Between 2000 and 3000 railwaymen and families were relocated to Eastleigh, altering the social fabric of Battersea.

161. *John Burns, MP for Battersea, addressing an open-air audience in 1897. Painting by A.J. Finberg.*

JOHN BURNS

Inextricably linked with the politics and trade union activities of Battersea was John Burns (1858-1943). Born in south Lambeth (though he often claimed to have been born in Battersea), Burns left school at the age of ten, and found employment at Price's candle factory before becoming an apprentice engineer. He built upon a minimal education by attendance at night-school, and became a compelling orator. In 1889 he became a representative for Battersea on the newly-established London County Council. That was an eventful year for him, for he was in the news constantly as leader of the famous London docks strike *(see below)* in which he used his undoubted talents to secure the support of leading members of the establishment for the plight of London dockers. It was hardly surprising that he also became Member of Parliament for Battersea in 1892 standing as an independent labour candidate, though he was never to join the Independent Labour Party because he disliked its outright opposition to the Liberal Party and he did not get on with Keir Hardie. He won the Battersea vote against the Conservative candidate by 5,616

to 4,057. As with his reluctance to join the ILP, although he attended the conference in 1900 which set up the Labour Party, he did not become a Labour Party candidate.

With continuing Progressive *(see p.129)* backing, Burns entered the Liberal Cabinet in 1906. Despite active hostility to him by suffragettes and some socialists, he was re-elected in 1910 with his largest vote, but only on a small majority due to a national swing to the Unionists. However, he did not fit easily into the Liberal camp just as he had not easily sat down with some of the more militant Socialist allies of his time. He had also enraged the public of Battersea in 1900 when, at the height of patriotic fervour for the Boer War, he had declared against it – he only just held on to his seat at the election that year.

Burns resigned his Cabinet post in 1914 because of his opposition to declaring war on Germany. He remained an MP until 1918, and decided not to accept the offer of candidacy from the newly formed Battersea Trades Council and Labour Party (see below). He went into retirement. Aided by a 5000 dollar bequest from the will of the philanthropist Andrew Carnegie, he devoted the

162. A Punch cartoon of John Burns, in December 1909.

rest of his long life to collecting books on London and on trade union history. His London collection was eventually presented to the London County Council and formed the basis of what is now the London Metropolitan Archives.

Burns married the daughter of a Battersea shipwright, and is buried in St Mary's churchyard.

STRIKES

In 1888 the success of the Bryant & May matchgirls' strike in the East End, to which John Burns gave his support, sparked an unprecedented wave of union organisation from 1889 to 1892, especially among the unskilled. In Battersea, different sections of workers founded local branch unions and won improvements in wages, hours and conditions for bakers, gasworkers, dockers, tramwaymen and barge builders.When a director of Morgan Crucible discovered a recruiting leaflet on the factory floor in 1890 for the Factory Operatives' & General Labourers' Union, the company implemented a reduction in hours to 54 within the month and in the following year introduced holiday pay.

The national dock strike of August and September of 1889 was vigorously led by Burns. After a collection in Australia raised £30,000 that saved the strike from collapse, the dockers eventually got an increase in pay. The strike spread further than the London docks to Nine Elms station, which was the destination for large quantities of coal from the Marquis of Londonderry's collieries in the north. Here, the team unloading vessels crucial to the supply of fuel to the Nine Elms gasworks, also went on strike for extra pay.

The first meeting of the National Union of Gas Workers and General Labourers was held at Battersea Park gates, with John Burns helping to organise branches at Vauxhall and at Nine Elms. Many of the national unions were founded by Battersea activists, for instance the Navvies', Bricklayers' Labourers' and General Labourers' Union and the National Federation of Labour Unions, with victory meetings gathering at Battersea Park gates afterwards.

A national railway strike in 1911 was supported by the Battersea railway unions and again during the 1926 National General Strike.

FRIENDLY SOCIETIES

A significant feature of Battersea life from the middle of the 19th century was the friendly society movement. The societies had intriguing names such as the Ancient Order of Foresters, the Independent Order of Oddfellows (Manchester Unity), the United Order of Ancient Druids and the Independent Order of Rechabites. Essentially voluntary benefit societies in which members contributed to a common fund to provide financial payments at times of sickness or death, the Orders grew to be the predominant form of friendly society in England.

Each had varying fortunes. Court 'Friend In Need' never got off the ground, probably due to the fact that Chatham Road, in the mid 1860s, was an isolated development, far from built up. Court 'Banks of the Thames' survived into the 20th century, with nearly 300 members during the 1870s and 1890s. The Court 'Flower of Surrey' was a female only Court, established as part of an initiative that began in the early 1890s to attract women to join the Foresters. By then many employers and trade unions were operating sickness funds and the Foresters' impact was limited. In addition one court moved into the parish to establish itself ultimately as 'Battersea Court'.

The longest lasting Foresters' Court to meet in

163. The Peabody Estate Office on the Shaftesbury Estate, 2002.

Battersea was Court 'Hospitality', No. 2226, originally meeting in Pimlico; it moved to Battersea about 1900. Despite the impact of the National Insurance Act of 1911, Court 'Hospitality' continued to flourish throughout the 20th century.

SHAFTESBURY PARK

Political involvement in the formation and management of housing estates can be clearly demonstrated with the Shaftesbury Park Estate. The Poupart market garden farm was sold to the Artizans' and General Labourers' Dwelling Company for development of the estate. The Company had been founded in 1867 by a group of workers to provide good quality housing for the working class; it identified itself with the co-operative movement and regularly advertised in the *Beehive* and the *Co-operator* newspapers. William Swindlehurst, the secretary, had been involved in the Preston branch of the Chartist Land Co. in 1848 and in 1858 had been the secretary of the Wandsworth Workingmen's Co-operative. Support was obtained from the Earl of Shaftesbury who laid the first stone in 1872 of the 1,100-house estate, from which beerhouses and taverns were excluded.

The development of Shaftesbury Park was crucial to Battersea's political development for it

attracted some of the better paid, and more radical artisans. Swindlehurst himself lived on the estate and became involved in organising activities. Other radical residents included the printer J.C. Durant, John Vooght, previously a member of the Clapham Vestry in the 1860s, George Harris and William Willis. Swindlehurst was convicted of fraud in 1877 over a land deal in North London.

Even though Parliamentary rules denied many on the estate from voting in elections, the tenants showed their political preferences during the 1880 parliamentary election when they used a Conservative election meeting to overwhelmingly endorse the Liberal candidates. In December 1883 the Shaftesbury Park Club and Institute was established under the leadership of Vooght, later moving to Lavender Hill where it has remained. The estate by the mid-1880s had a complexity of organisations including a Band of Hope, a Dramatic Club, a Friends of Labour Loan Society, rifle corps, sports team, an annual flower show and a Lodge of the Good Templars. After a co-operative store on the estate failed in 1881, the premises were taken over by the Battersea and Wandsworth Co-operative Society (founded 1854 at Price's Candles) which later transferred the business onto Lavender Hill.

The Twentieth Century

A RADICAL COUNCIL

The Progressives (a shifting alliance of trade unionists, socialists, radicals, liberals and temperance and free church activists) who had control of the Vestry and Council for fifteen years up to 1909 and from 1912 to 1919, when it was replaced by the Labour Party, used the municipal machinery for the benefit of its working-class electoral roll. Building work was undertaken by direct labour rather than by private contractors; wage levels were increased and weekly hours reduced to 48. A Council depot was opened in 1898 with a joiner's shop, wheelwright's shop, and a blacksmith and fitter's shop, with stabling for four horses. The Council's motto, adopted in 1900, was *Non mihi, non tibi, sed nobis*; the translation reads, 'Neither for you, nor for me, but for us'.

The Borough Council instigated the construction of low cost housing on its Latchmere estate of 315 houses and flats in 1903 and soon built the Town Hall Dwellings of 18 tenements of two flats providing a total of 351 housing units. During the 1930s, larger blocks of five to six storeys were built on the St John's Estate, Vicarage Crescent and Stewarts Lane Estate.

Council members were on the radical side of politics, supporting Irish independence, the National Stop the War Committee against the 1899-1902 Boer War: Joubert Street, on the newly completed Latchmere Estate, was named after one of the leading Boer generals. In 1902 the Council declined to sign a loyal address on Edward VII's coronation. Britain's first black mayor of a metropolitan borough was John Archer, a photographer. His election as mayor took place on 10 November 1913 when, as a member of the majority Progressive Party, 30 votes were cast in his favour and 29 for his opponent. From 1918 until his death in 1932 he was a Councillor, Alderman and leading member of Battersea Trades Council and Labour Party.

Charlotte Despard, novelist and suffragette, was an early member of the Battersea Trades Council and Labour Party, funding premises and staff for the newly formed Battersea Labour Party in 1918/9. She was also the leader of the Women's Freedom League and prominent in calling for school meals.

The North Battersea constituency in 1922 voted

164. Charlotte Despard, c.1908

165. Shapurji Saklatvala.

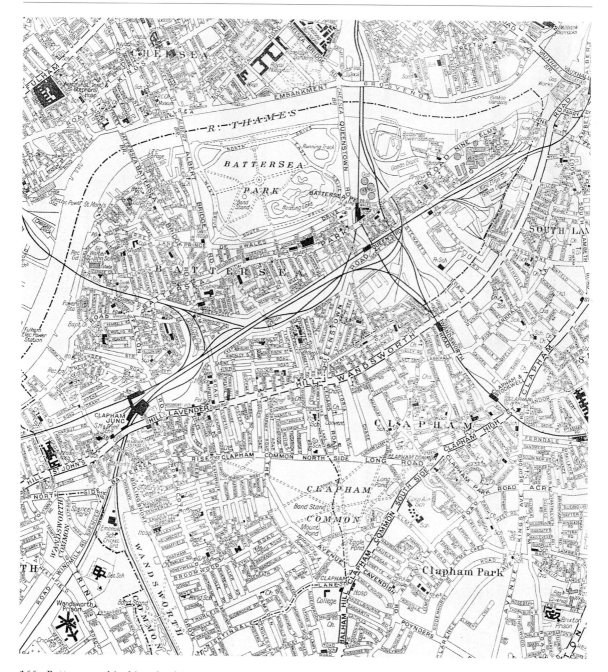

166. *Battersea and its hinterland in 1922.*

167. *A group of ladies about to board a charabanc for a day trip c.1930. They were setting out from Henry Street, later renamed Winders Road, off Castle Street.*

168. *Electric House, Lavender Hill, decorated and illuminated for the Jubilee of King George V in 1935.*

169. Painting of the Battersea Rise and Northcote Road junction entitled 'Crossroads from my Window', 1932.

in a communist labour candidate, the Indian Shapurji Saklatvala, who lost the seat in 1923 but was returned again in 1924. Writing to an Irish self-determination group in 1923 he said: "The British Empire is made up of the aristocratic and cunning 'dirty dogs' of Great Britain, who will assail any country at any time… to retain all the stolen property and to keep under bondage all the bullied nations". Following the ban on communists as Labour Party members, the Labour candidate, Stephen Sanders, replaced Saklatvala in 1929.

The American Singer, Paul Robeson, appeared at Battersea Town Hall in November 1937, at a concert to celebrate the 20th anniversary of the founding of the Soviet Union.

Battersea Council objected in the early 1920s to the British Broadcasting Corporation using the initials BBC because they thought confusion might reign. Wireless was then in its infancy and the Council must have considered itself as more likely to be important.

THE SECOND WORLD WAR

The Second World War had a devastating impact on Battersea with whole streets in Nine Elms, off Thessaly Road and Stewarts Road blasted by landmines and continual bombing during the Blitz and after. The area had many likely targets – the railway yards, bridges and viaducts, power station and vast tracts of industry. Many local landmarks were destroyed: Christchurch, the Pavilion cinema and Shakespeare Theatre on Lavender Hill, the fire station in Battersea Park Road, the Surrey Hounds public house on St John's Hill and Battersea railway station in the High Street were just a few of the many.

In Battersea 3,000 houses were demolished or considered a total loss and virtually every house suffered damage – 22,000 had been repaired up to 1948.

170. Christchurch, Battersea Park Road, after being struck by a V2 rocket, 21 November 1944.

TERRITORIALS

In February 1951 a Deputy Lieutenant of London's committee was formed in Battersea for the purpose of promoting local enthusiasm for a local Territorial Army unit. This arose from proposals advanced in the Greater London Development Plan. At that time there was only the one Battersea Territorial unit, the 42nd Royal Tank Regiment, RAC (TA) with its headquarters at 27 St John's Hill, although a second unit, the No 8 Platoon 'C' Company, 327th Battalion, Women's Royal Army Corps, (TA) was in the process of being formed.

The 42nd had a long and distinguished history. Its lineal ancestor was the Newington Surrey Volunteers, one of many armed associations formed at the end of the 18th century when a wave of patriotism swept the countryside, inspiring the British to take measures for protection from a threatened invasion by a French fleet. The threat passed, but the regiment continued under a variety of names, to be called up for duty in the wars of the 20th century. It first saw action in 1900 when it supplied a Company to the 2nd Battalion the East Surrey Regiment in the South African War. During the Great War, now restyled the 23rd London Regiment, it provided two Bat-

171. The aftermath of a V1 flying bomb that destroyed the Surrey Hounds public house, St John's Hill, and a passing bus, causing many casualties, 17 June 1944.

172. The brick dump at Thessaly Road, where rubble was accumulated from numerous bombing incidents, c.1946.

In 1938, after 140 years as an infantry unit, the regiment was converted to armour and became the 42nd Battalion Royal Tank Corps. When war came in 1939, training was still in the elementary stages and equipment was limited and primitive. By the end of 1940 however the regiment was fully equipped with Matilda tanks and in the spring of 1941 it was despatched as part of the 1st Army Tank Brigade to the Middle East. After a lengthy spell of active service it returned home in preparation for the Normandy landings. Although being sent to Normandy the unit, due to its speciality in night operations, was not called upon and in October was temporarily disbanded and its personnel transferred to other units. After the war the 42nd was reformed as a Territorial Armoured Regiment in the London Armoured Division.

talions for service abroad. The 1st Battalion served continuously in France from March 1915 until the Armistice. The 2nd Battalion went to France in 1916, then proceeded to Macedonia, took part in Allenby's campaign in Palestine and finished up in Flanders in 1918. Twenty-five official battle honours were awarded for their campaigns and are carried on the regimental colours.

REHOUSING
The LCC and Battersea Borough Council cleared away many older houses and redeveloped large areas in the 1960s and 1970s with multi-storey blocks on the Surrey Lane, York Road, Battersea Park Road and Doddington Road Estates.

In all this, tightly-knit communities based in

173. Battersea High Street in July 1962, shortly before demolition of the 17th-century Castle public house.

174. Pavilion Chambers and Lavenham Court, Lavender Hill, the 1960s' replacement for the shopping parade destroyed in 1944.

Battersea were torn from their surroundings and dispersed into large blocks of flats in Roehampton and elsewhere in the 1950s and 1960s.

THE FESTIVAL OF BRITAIN

Part of Battersea Park was chosen as the site for the frivolous side to the Festival of Britain of 1951. The residents of the large mansion flats in Prince of Wales Drive signed an unsuccessful petition against the Festival Gardens and funfair but they opened on 3 May to popular acclaim. There were a variety of pavilions for dancing, theatre, ballet, and various eating and drinking establishments. For the children a Punch and Judy show was put on each day, and in the Riverside theatre, Britain's leading puppet makers gave a daytime show. Each evening had a fireworks display. Donkey, baby elephant and pony rides were an added attraction at the children's zoo and pets' corner. The LCC also staged a modern sculpture exhibition within the park.

The first season of the Festival Gardens, up to 3 November 1951, saw 7,750,000 visitors and by popular demand they were reopened the following year. Among the favourite attractions were the Guinness Clock, The Emmett Railway and the

175. Construction under way in March 1956 of a new housing development, the Battersea Park Estate off Battersea Park Road.

176. *The Tree Walk at the Festival Pleasure Gardens, Battersea Park c.1951.*

Tree Walk. The attractions of the funfair contained a Big Dipper, Dragon Ride, Three Abreast Gallopers, The Whip, Dodgems, Ghost Train, Hurricane ride, Moon Rocket etc. The rides at the funfair were to change each year as attractions were alternated with those from seaside resorts and continued in operation until 1974.

SOCIAL CHANGE
The major change to Battersea since the 1950s has been the run down and removal of nearly all the riverside industries and the land reused either for housing or commercial offices. Retail development at the Clapham Junction approach and the Asda superstore on Lavender Hill took place during the 1980s. Many more restaurants and fast food eating establishments have appeared during the 1980s and 1990s, altering the social standing of the area and the once thriving street markets in the High Street and Northcote Road have declined. The architectural heritage of the Victorian housing has been preserved in schemes, such as the conservation order placed on the

Shaftesbury Estate in 1976, and the central shopping district of Clapham Junction has been designated as a Conservation Area, with schemes in place to reintroduce some of the Victorian architectural design features to the shop facades.

The proposed £500 million redevelopment of the area surrounding and including the Battersea Power Station by Parkview International includes: a sports 'infotainment' venue, a custom designed theatre for Cirque du Soleil, retail units, bars, cafés, restaurants and a 24-hour, 16-screen cinema. It is planned to include also a 400-room hotel, a 700-room business and conference hotel and a 650-unit residential accommodation. The plans feature a new rail terminus to provide a shuttle service from Victoria Station and a new dedicated river bus service. Further plans are to redevelop the former railway yards between the Victoria Railway Bridge and Chelsea Bridge.

The tallest building in Battersea, apart from the long defunct Power Station, was completed in 2000/2001, the Montevetro apartment block at 112 Battersea Church Road, which overshadows

the parish church of St Mary. It replaced the Rank Hovis flourmill, demolished a few years earlier. The Richard Rogers Partnership designed the glass-clad, wedge-shaped complex in 1994. The building has received a mixed reaction with the Civic Trust giving a 'commendation' only, not offering any awards for the design. The 20 floors of the tower, reaching a height of 211 feet, contain 103 apartments, ranging in price from £465,000 for a 2-bedroom unit to £5 million for the Duplex apartment on the 18/19 floors. The private gardens include a tennis court and leisure centre.

The disappearance of riverside wharves between Battersea Park and the old Battersea village, and their replacement by residential apartments will remove further the chance of industry or of local employment reviving. Industry now in Battersea is probably at the same level as it was in the 17th century.

177. The Montevetro apartment block in Battersea Church Road, adjacent to the old parish church of St Mary in 2002. The oppressive tower blocks to the right were erected by the Borough Council.

178. The Westland Heliport at Lombard Road, 5 April 1965.

Famous Names

William Wilberforce (1759-1833), MP for Hull and later for the county of Yorkshire, was closely associated with the younger Pitt. He held strong religious views, founding the Proclamation Society in 1787 for the suppression of vice and becoming the leading light of the evangelical Clapham Sect. He spent much of his time from 1792 at Battersea Rise House with his friend **Henry Thornton** and from 1796, when he married, until 1807 at a house called Broomfield, where Broomwood Road was later developed. He had devoted much of his time to the abolition of slavery and finally saw a Bill passed in 1807. Broomfield House was demolished in 1904 and a blue plaque was put up on 111 Broomwood Road.

The founder of *The Times* newspaper, **John Walter** (1739-1812), lived at Gilmore House, Clapham Common, North Side from 1773 to 1783. A GLC blue plaque records his time here. Residents of the house also included Mrs Gilmore (Isabella Morris, sister of William Morris) and Mrs Seline Grote, mother of George Grote, historian and politician. The Clapham Sect met in the house.

George Alfred Henty (1832-1902) lived at 33 Lavender Gardens. He was a well-respected correspondent covering the Crimean war and reported on wars in Italy, Serbia and Abysinnia. His novels include titles such as *With Wolfe in Canada*, *The Dash for Khartoum* and *The Cornet of Horse* after which a pub in Lavender Gardens is named. A blue plaque in his memory has been placed on 33 Lavender Gardens.

Edward Thomas (1878-1917), essayist and poet, was educated at Battersea Grammar School and lived at 61 Shelgate Road and elsewhere in Battersea. He wrote essays and poems on the countryside and gained a reputation as a war poet but was killed in action in 1917. A blue plaque was placed on the Shelgate Road address.

The political giant of Battersea, **John Burns** (1858-1943) lived at 110 Clapham Common North Side from 1914 until his death. His political career is dealt with briefly on page 126.

Tom Taylor (1817-1880) dramatist, art critic, civil servant, barrister and editor of *Punch* magazine, lived in a mansion on Lavender Sweep from 1859 until his death. He wrote in 1858 the play *Our American Cousin* – the one that President Lincoln was watching when shot on 14 April 1865.

Richard Church, (1893–1972) novelist, writer of travel books and literary critic described his early life in Battersea in his book *Over the Bridge*.

179. *The Thornton family home, Battersea Rise House, where meetings of the Clapham Sect took place, and where William Wilberforce stayed at times from 1792.*

George Shearing, the jazz pianist, arranger and composer was born, congenitally blind, in Battersea in 1919. He studied music for four years at the Linden Lodge School for the Blind at the corner of Dents Road and Bolingbroke Grove. Moving to America in 1947 he formed his own jazz quintet and became famous for the classic *Lullaby of Birdland*. Awarded many accolades, including a youth community centre named after him in Este Road, he received an OBE in 1996.

The comic actor, **Wally Patch** (1888-1970) also came from Battersea. He appeared in many films, mainly comedies, such as *Busman's Holiday* (1936), *Bank Holiday* (1938), *History of Mr Polly*, *George in Civvy Street*, George Formby's last film (1946), *The Adventures of Jane* (1949), *I'm Alright Jack* with Peter Sellers (1959), *Poor Cow* (1968) and many more.

Don Cockell was born in Battersea on 22 September 1922. His boxing career began in 1946 and he went on to win the British and European light heavyweight title in 1951, British and Empire light-heavy weight titles in 1952 and British and Empire heavyweight titles in 1953 and 1954. He travelled to the USA in 1955 in an attempt to take Rocky Marciano's World title from him but was stopped in the ninth round. Marciano said after the fight, "He's got a lot of guts. I don't think I ever hit anyone else any more often or harder." Don retired from boxing in 1956 and died in 1983.

The guitarist and lutenist, **Julian Bream**, was born in Battersea on 15 July 1933. He learned to play the guitar from his father. He won a scholarship to the Royal College of Music, made his debut at Cheltenham in 1947 and took part in dozens of BBC broadcasts by his sixteenth birthday. He has become famous for his solo guitar and lute recitals of contemporary and classical music. Bream founded the Julian Bream Concert in 1960 and in 1961 established the Semley Festival in Wiltshire for rare chamber music. He was awarded an OBE in 1964 for services to music, the CBE in 1985 and Honorary Doctorates from the Universities of Surrey and Leeds. He was elected an Honorary Member of the Royal Academy of Music in 1966 and a Fellowship of the Royal College of Music in 1981. His recordings have sold by the million and RCA presented him with a platinum disc in 1979 to mark record sales of half a million in the UK alone.

180. George Alfred Henty.

Edward Adrian Wilson (1872-1912) lived at St Mary's House, Vicarage Crescent in the 1890s. Doctor, naturalist and explorer, he accompanied Robert Scott on his tragic journey during 1911-1912 to the South Pole and his body was discovered alongside that of Scott and Bowers. A blue plaque has been erected on St Mary's House to his memory.

The novelist and author, **G.K. Chesterton** lived at 60 Overstrand Mansions, Prince of Wales Drive from 1903 to 1907, and then at no. 48 until 1910.

Albert Mansbridge founded the Workers' Educational Association and was instrumental in forming the National Central Library, now part of the British Library. He was educated at Sir Walter St John's School and spent his early years in Battersea Bridge Road.

While writing the novel *Up the Junction* about a group of young girls working in a sweet factory, **Nell Dunn** and her husband, Jeremy Sandford, lived in Lavender Road.

Bibliography

All About Battersea, Henry S. Simmons (1882)
The Almshouses of London, Clive Berridge (1987)
Amber Valley Gazetteer of Greater London's Cinemas, Malcolm Webb (1986)
Battersea Borough Guides
Historic Battersea, Sherwood Ramsey (1913)
The Story of Battersea, E.A. Woolmer (1923)
The Pleasure Gardens, Battersea Park Guide (1951)
Battersea and Clapham, Images of England, P. Loobey (1994, revised 1996)
Battersea and Clapham, Images of England, A second selection, P. Loobey (2000)
Battersea Park, an Illustrated History, Friends of Battersea Park (1993)
Battersea Park as a centre for Nature Study, Walter Johnson FGS (1910)
Battersea Power Station, London Power Co. and CEGB (Various dates)
Battersea New Town 1790-1870, Keith Bailey (1980)
Battersea Works, The Morgan Crucible Co. Ltd, 1856-1956
Our Lady of Batersey, J.G. Taylor (1925)
Marc Isambard Brunel, P. Clements (1970)
Building Cycles and Britain's Growth, J Parry Lewis (1965)
Change at Clapham Junction – The railways of Wandsworth and South West London, Tim Sherwood (1994)
Clapham Past, Gillian Glegg (1998)
Thomas Cubitt, Master Builder, Hermione Hobhouse (1971)
Flights of Fancy, Early Aviation in Battersea and Wandsworth, P. Loobey (1981)
For love and shillings, Wandsworth women's working lives, Jo Stanley & Bronwen Griffiths (1990)
The Illustrated Omnibus Guide (No 1, May 1851 repr. 1971)
Inn and around London, A history of Young's Pubs, Helen Osborn (1991)
Life and Labour of the People in London 17 vols, Charles Booth (1892 to 1902)
London County Council Tramways, Vol. 1, E.R. Oakley (1971)
London South of the Thames, Walter Besant (1912)
London Theatres and Music Halls, 1850-1950, Diana Howard (1970)
The Metamorphosis of Battersea (OU unpubl. thesis), Keith Bailey (1995)
A Morning's walk from London to Kew, Sir R. Phillips (1817)
The Park Town Estate and the Battersea Tangle, Priscilla Metcalf (1978)

Putney and Roehampton Past, Dorian Gerhold (1994)
Reflections on Battersea, Rotary Club of Battersea (1980)
Reflections on Battersea, Book Two, Rotary Club of Battersea (1981)
Royal River Highway, F.L. Dix (1985)
A History of Sir Walter St John's School, 1700-1986, Frank T. Smallwood (1998)
South Battersea, The Formative Years 1851-1900, Roger Logan (1977)
The Speculative Builders and Developers of Victorian London, H.J. Dyos (1968)
The Thames – The Waterway of the World, Stratten & Stratten (1893)
Tramways in Wandsworth and Battersea, C.S. Dunbar (1971)
Wandsworth Historian, Journal of the Wandsworth Historical Society
Wandsworth Past, Dorian Gerhold (1998)
We Served: War-Time, Battersea and Wandsworth 1939-1945, Tony Shaw (1989)
Wellington, A personal history, Christopher Hibbert (1997)
The Boroughs of Wandsworth & Battersea at War, P. Loobey (1996)
The Buildings of Clapham, The Clapham Society (2000)

JOURNALS AND NEWSPAPERS
The Builder
The Graphic
Illustrated London News
South Western Star
Wandsworth Borough News
Wandsworth, Battersea District Times
South London Press
The Times

The chief sources for historical material on Battersea have been the following, where a wealth of material in the form of books, pamphlets, maps, newspapers, planning applications, local directories, rate books, photographs, prints, Borough guides, invoices, voting lists, manorial court rolls and of course the census returns are available to researchers:

Lambeth Archives at the Minet Library
The British Library
The Guildhall Library
The London Metropolitan Archives
Northamptonshire Record Office
Public Record Office, Kew.
Wandsworth Museum
Wandsworth Local History Collection, Battersea Library.